Serving
with Eyes
Wide Open

Serving with Eyes Wide Open

Doing Short-Term Missions with Cultural Intelligence

David A. Livermore

BakerBooks

Grand Rapids, Michigan

© 2006 by David A. Livermore

Published by Baker Books
a division of Baker Publishing Group
P.O. Box 6287, Grand Rapids, MI 49516-6287
www.bakerbooks.com

Printed in the United States of America

Library of Congress Cataloging-in-Publication Data
Livermore, David A., 1967-
  Serving with eyes wide open : doing short-term missions with cultural
intelligence / David A. Livermore.
      p.   cm.
  Includes bibliographical references (p.   ).
  ISBN 10: 0-8010-6616-6
  ISBN 978-0-8010-6616-0
  1. Short-term missions. I. Title.
BV2082.S56L59 2006
266'.02373—dc22   2005032197

10   11   12   13   14   15   16   13   12   11   10   9   8

Contents

Foreword

I've had the privilege of knowing about Dave Livermore and ob-serving his dedication to cross-cultural ministry for more than a decade. Like many of the early devotees of short-term missions, especially trips involving young people, Dave's interest in and commitment to short-term missions started with a view that focused primarily on giving Western Christians a great cross-cultural experience to foster their own growth.

In the late twentieth century, churches across America (and other wealthier nations) jumped at this unprecedented oppor-tunity created by the advent of long-haul travel to go, minister, and learn in a fascinating world of cultures and adventures. Short-term missions morphed from a primary avenue for mis-sionary recruitment to a foundational assumption for provoking spiritual growth in the lives of the participants.

Thankfully, Dave did not stay locked in this "missions for the benefit of me" mind-set. His long-term dedication to listening to and learning from brothers and sisters in the non-Western world transformed his perspective into what is now a commitment to genuine cross-cultural relationships and effective partnerships with the church in the majority world.

I finally met Dave personally when he was well into this jour-ney, and I deeply appreciated his willingness to be self-critical, to ask tough questions about some of our culturally insensitive assumptions, and to practice what he preaches in this book. He has slowed down, put his passport on the shelf for a while, and asked questions about rethinking and reworking short-term missions.

This book is the result of his reflection and research. It will serve well any leader who is willing to ask questions about how short-term missions can best serve the global advancement of Christ's kingdom—and not just the experiential advancement of Christians who are wealthy enough to participate in global adventures.

Dave's global overviews, careful research, and practical tools combine his skills as a youth worker, missiologist, and anthropologist. Like a news reporter in the helicopter above the highway, Dave gives us the "skyway patrol" view of short-term missions. While we are celebrating the sheer volume of short-term mission's traffic, Dave takes time to give us a sense of the road ahead. He warns us of the culturally insensitive potholes that could keep us from joining the mainstream of God's activity in the majority world. He gives voice to non-Western leaders so that we don't continue on the road to ineffectiveness. And he points us in a direction that will keep us from taking the wrong exit, a detour into our own cultural self-absorption caused by our failure to evaluate our basic assumptions and listen to our non-Western cotravelers.

Like Dave, I believe in short-term missions, and I encourage churches and ministries to get involved. But I also believe that our Western approach to short-term missions, behavior in relating to those from other cultures, and perspective on the purposes of short-term missions desperately needs an overhaul and a reevaluation. *Serving with Eyes Wide Open: Doing Short-Term Missions with Cultural Intelligence* provokes this overhaul. Any leader who is willing to take time to reflect on where short-term missions fit in our Western contribution to global Christianity will find this book an essential resource.

Paul Borthwick, Development Associates International,
author of *A Mind for Missions:*
Ten Ways to Build Your World Vision

Acknowledgments

First and foremost, I'm grateful to my non-Western friends scattered in places all around the world who have confided in me the joys and challenges of interacting with the North American church, including me. One of my driving agendas in this book is to allow more Americans to hear their voice.

In addition, I'm extremely grateful for the encouragement and support of Grand Rapids Theological Seminary and, in particular, our president, Dr. Doug Fagerstrom. Doug has not only been supportive of my pursuing this project but has held me accountable for protecting the time needed to get it done.

My ministry partner and lifelong friend Steve Argue has listened to countless rants as I worked through this material. He continually sharpens my thinking and living in ways he'll never realize.

Bob Hosack, the chief acquisitions editor for Baker Books and my new friend, has been nothing but stellar in the encouragement, feedback, and direction he's provided me along with the rest of his team at Baker.

And most of all, I'm grateful to my precious daughters, Emily and Grace, and my soul mate and wife, Linda. Not only did they give me the needed space to write, but they embrace the globe with me, even when they stay home and I travel apart from them. I'm not worthy of you dear women!

Soli deo gloria.

Introduction

On a cool November evening in London, I was roaming the winding streets of Piccadilly Circus with my African friend Mark. This was Mark's first trip out of Africa. Experiencing the multisensory experience of the night scene in Piccadilly Circus with him is a memory I'll never forget. It was the perfect way to view a culture—Mark and I each coming from unique cultural vantage points. I also will never forget our topic of conversation that evening. We had just finished dinner and an orientation meeting with a group of American[1] youth pastors who had just arrived for a two-week mission trip during which they would conduct youth ministry training in several churches throughout Europe.

Mark said, "Dave, that group was just so American!"

"Wait a minute. You're talking to a full-blooded American!" I replied.

For the time being, he assured me, I was exempt from his tirade against Americans. "They didn't ask me a single question all night long," he continued. "They were loud and brash. And they have prepared for this trip just enough to make them dangerous."

Mark's first two accusations were nothing new to me. I had observed and heard those criticisms all too often about my culture. However his concern about preparation making them dangerous intrigued me. I've spent the last several years moving in and out of a lot of different cultures. I've participated in and led dozens of short-term mission trips, and I've always made preparation and orientation nonnegotiable. Still, was Mark on to something? Could preparation actually hinder one's engagement in being effective cross-culturally?

Cross-cultural encounters used to be reserved for an elite few jet-setters who constantly cross continental lines. Today, however, they're an everyday part of our lives. The American pastors who joined us in London are among millions of Americans who participate in short-term mission trips each year. Some estimate that as many as four million Americans take short-term mission trips out of the country annually; and American churches now spend as much on short-term mission trips as on long-term missionaries.[2]

Add to the ever-growing mission trip "industry" the business travelers who hop between Montreal, London, Beijing, and Sydney like we used to move from state to state, or province to province. International travel is at an all-time high. You don't even have to travel outside your own town to encounter the phenomenon of people living on opposite sides of the world but linked in ways previously unimaginable. Sitting at home in St. Louis, you can play chess on the Internet with someone in China.

Even in sleepy, Midwest cities like Grand Rapids, Michigan, where I live, cross-cultural encounters abound. Just this morning I stopped at the grocery store, where a Sudanese man who arrived here a few months ago checked out my items. A couple hours later, I made a phone call to my credit-card company and ended up being routed to a call center in New Delhi, India. At lunch I overheard the couple behind me at the restaurant talking about their trip to Capetown, South Africa, next week. When I returned to my office, I opened the Internet browser on my computer. It defaults to BBC News, so I was immediately viewing images from Gaza, North Korea, England, Nepal, and more—all accompanied by current updates! I have more up-to-date information on what's happening in Gaza right now than on how my girls are doing at school today. Cross-cultural encounters are all around us.

Neither my parents nor my in-laws have ever had a passport. I don't expect they ever will. However, each of my girls has one, and they're still in elementary school. The vast majority of the students at the seminary where I teach not only have passports but have multiple stamps throughout them. We've never had greater accessibility and opportunity to cross over cultural lines, whether in our own backyards or twelve time zones away. We're traveling as never before.

Sadly, however, our increased accessibility to the globe doesn't seem to have dwindled our colonialist[3] tendencies. Much of the way we interact cross-culturally continues to be filled with an "Our way is best" mentality. The importance of cross-cultural sensitivity and awareness of different cultures is certainly better than a couple decades ago. However, a subtle sense among Americans that we have the "right" culture and thus need to "convert" others to our ways still permeates much of our cross-cultural perspective and practice—whether it's work we're doing as part of a multinational corporation, a university study-abroad program, or a mission trip.

This book is an attempt to open our eyes to existing blind spots in global missions, specifically short-term missions. I want to change the way we *see* and therefore *do* short-term missions. My own cross-cultural work has often reflected the weaknesses described in this book, so I do not write as one who embodies the perfect approach to cross-cultural interaction. However, exposure to my own neocolonialism and that of others has transformed the way I interact cross-culturally. Just as important, it's altered my perspective of myself, of others, of the world, and of my faith.

That's what I desire in writing this book—that we pause long enough amid our life in a global village to see what we may have missed before. I call us to question our assumptions, to hear the voices of non-Westerners who have received our mission trips, our consulting, and our training modules. I want us to be open to the idea that our overall perspective might need altering.

This book is for anyone who wants to be more effective cross-culturally—whether in preparing you for your upcoming mission trip or tour abroad, helping you relate to an immigrant at work, or enhancing the work you do overseas as part of your job. *Serving with Eyes Wide Open* also is a resource for churches, mission agencies, universities, and other parachurch agencies that continually grapple with the issues of cross-cultural interactions. While the book was written with that kind of broad audience in mind, the focus is particularly upon those who engage in short-term mission trips—either at home or abroad. In addition to the millions of Americans going overseas on short-term mission trips, as many or more participate in cross-cultural projects at home in their own communities and nearby states. The material in this book applies to both international and domestic cross-cultural encounters.

The short-term mission industry has huge buy-in from other Western[4] nations as well, including places like Canada, the United Kingdom, Australia, and Singapore. My own research has focused primarily upon those of us from the United States, and in some cases Canada, who participate in cross-cultural mission work. However, my friends from other Western nations tell me much of what's reported here also applies to their cross-cultural practice, though I can't begin to assume its relevance beyond my own context.

Due to the ever-growing numbers of people doing short-term mission work abroad, an increasing number of resources are available to assist in these endeavors. Some helpful works deal specifically with the logistics and planning of such trips. Other more technical and scholarly works take a strongly theoretical approach to intercultural practice, and still others a more devotional approach to short-term missions and its transformational impact on the participants. Many of these are worthwhile resources, some of which I've included in the appendix.

This book, while being informed by those other helpful resources, takes a different approach—specifically examining the perspectives and assumptions we bring into our cross-cultural practices. The biggest problems in short-term missions are not technical or administrative. The biggest challenges lie in communication, misunderstanding, personality conflict, poor leadership, and bad teamwork. All too often we try to respond to these challenges by attempting to change surface-level behaviors rather than getting at the assumptions and convictions behind our behaviors. We learn the dos and don'ts about how to act when we go somewhere, yet it seems to make little difference in how we actually interact cross-culturally. We come home with zealous descriptions of how we've changed, yet within a few weeks, our lives look pretty identical to how they looked before the trip.

Serving with Eyes Wide Open is an attempt to open our eyes and see what we might otherwise miss. It's my belief that as we do so, we'll not only interact in more Christ-honoring ways but also come away with a higher degree of lasting change in us and in the church of Jesus Christ as a whole.

Another priority of this book is to give voice to non-Western church leaders from a variety of settings. These brothers and sisters are on the receiving end of our short-term mission projects. Many of them are too gracious to state overtly some of the things they've confided in me as I've spent the last several years researching short-term mission projects. It's my hope that this book is one small step forward in listening to the global church, of which the American church is now a small minority.

Finally, this book is unique in that it applies CQ, the theory of *cultural intelligence*, to missions. IQ, or intelligence quotient, is a concept we all understand. For years we've heard of people with really high IQs as compared to the rest of us with average levels of intelligence. In more recent years, psychologists have taught us about the importance of EQ, a measurement of how well we're in tune with our emotions. CQ simply draws upon some of the same ideas and research in measuring our ability to interact cross-culturally.[5]

There are three parts to the book. Part 1 gives a wide-angle view on our twenty-first-century world and church. We live in a global village, and awareness of the pressing issues of our village is an important springboard for a discussion about cross-cultural encounters. In addition, the largest Christian communities today are not in the U.S. Bible Belt but in Africa and Latin America. We must stop to understand the changing face of Christianity if we are to appropriately see what we're joining when we engage in missions cross-culturally. "Serving with eyes wide open" begins with a widened perspective on the realities of our twenty-first-century world.

Part 2 explores the conflicting perspectives between Americans and the global church about short-term missions. It examines the assumptions that drive much of our cross-cultural work. The primary source of the information in these chapters is my original research on short-term missions. For example, I studied the practice of North American pastors who went overseas for ten days to two weeks to train national pastors. The research compared the North American pastors' assessment of their cross-cultural training efforts with that of the nationals who received the training. This, combined with research on short-term mis-

sions by others and me, and the literature of cross-cultural interactions as a whole, led to the six areas of conflicting perspectives
described in part 2. These realities permeate the assumptions of
our short-term work.

Part 3 provides a matrix for applying CQ to short-term work.
Parts 1 and 2 are meant to simply widen our perspective as we
think about short-term missions. The material in part 3, however,
helps us apply our widened perspective and actually *do* short-
term missions more effectively. We don't have to try to master
CQ before our next trip. Instead we want to embark on a lifelong
journey of using CQ to more effectively live out the most basic
commands given to us for use in both short-term missions and
our day-to-day living back home—the commands to love God
and love others.

It's an amazing privilege to interact with people from other
cultures, both in our own neighborhoods and on the other side of
the world. The 6.5 billion people around the world are so much
like us yet very different. May this book serve you and the church
of Jesus Christ as we seek to more accurately reflect God's glory
when encountering the diverse people with whom we share the
world. We will grapple with some hard-hitting realities in the
pages that follow, but I encourage you to persevere; that's not
the end of the story. I have great hope for the opportunities that
lie on the horizon as we increasingly become part of a transient,
global church traveling from everywhere to everywhere. Open
your eyes. There's much to see in the movement of short-term
missions, and more importantly, the movement of God in the
world at large. Thanks for embarking on this journey with me.

Part 1

Looking through a Wide-Angle Lens

Globalization and the Church

We begin our journey toward serving with eyes wide open by looking through a wide-angle lens at the twenty-first-century world. After surviving the Cold War, the nuclear arms race, two world wars, several genocide attempts, and numerous totalitarian regimes, we find ourselves in a new century. Americans in 1900 had a life expectancy of forty-seven, whereas today it's seventy-six. As a worldwide group of people, we've undergone immense change over the last century. The Christian church has been in a state of major transition as well—both local congregations and the church at large.

Widening our perspective on the world in which we live should be an ongoing process for all of us. The next two chapters present a few snapshots of our world—the world as a whole, and the worldwide church of Jesus Christ. Like any snapshot, these pictures give us only a glimpse into the realities behind the images. It's important we take the time to view them, however, before we jump into specifically thinking about short-term mission work. Grab a cup of coffee and take a quick tour with me around the world. Serving with eyes wide open starts with seeing the world in which we're serving with a wide-angle lens.

One World

Snapshots of the Globe

Rarely have I been as strongly impressed with the globalization of our twenty-first-century world than I was a few months ago in Seattle. My friend Tony, from Mexico City, was also visiting Seattle, and we agreed to meet for lunch. We met at an easy-to-find spot in Seattle's Chinatown and walked through the international district for a few minutes before ending up at a French café. We walked inside, and soon after we were seated, a Haitian woman came up to take our order. She suggested some English Breakfast tea with our entrées. As she took our order, a group of Japanese businessmen sat down at the table behind us. I looked at Tony and said, "Do you see what just happened? In a matter of three minutes, we've encountered Mexican, American, Chinese, French, Haitian, English, and Japanese cultures!" As a result, Tony and I launched into an interesting discussion about the twenty-first-century world in which we live. Experiencing a mosaic of cultures as Tony and I did that day used to be reserved for the jet-setting few who hung out in international airports. But the world is becoming increasingly smaller.

At the same time, Americans still fare poorly with regard to our awareness of what's going on in the world. Our collective global consciousness is pretty dismal, and the mainstream media do little to help. Our family often hosts international guests in our home, and our guests are forever frustrated that they can't get more than a passing glimpse of world events from our nightly news. Becoming globally conscious doesn't come easily. It requires extra effort on our part.

Think about how many Americans asked, "Why do they hate us so much?" after the September 11 attacks. The tragic events of September 11 and all that's ensued since are not just about oil prices or the United States's troubled relationship with the Middle East. Economic, political, legal, and cultural forces are involved, crossing geopolitical boundaries, creating international problems, and requiring international solutions. We are all citizens of a global world, whether or not we realize it.

A comprehensive review of the endless issues characterizing our world goes beyond the purposes of this book. However, our journey into widening our perspective on global missions begins by looking at some of the predominant issues facing our twenty-first-century world. While by no means an exhaustive list, some of the most important issues facing us include the following snapshots.

Snapshot 1: Growing Population of the World

Every second, four babies are born. Four more babies were just born . . . and four more . . . and four more . . . and four more. It continues day after day after day, the population of the world growing at a rapid rate. More than twice as many people are born each day than die. All this adds up to a world population of 6.5 billion people. Line us all up in single file around the world and we'd circle the globe more than 110 times. At this rate, we can expect a population of eight billion people by the year 2025.[1]

Where are all these people? Twenty percent live in China. Twenty percent live in India. Five percent live in the United States. Fifty-five percent live in the other nations of the world. Developing nations are growing rapidly while their industrialized neighbors remain relatively static. The 6.5 billion of us are scattered throughout approximately two hundred nations, but there are more than five thousand identifiable ethnocultural groups in the world.[2]

Nearly half the people in the world are children. Forty percent of the world is under fifteen, while less than 20 percent of Americans are under fifteen. Many of our global children have a dismal future. It's hard to grow up when you're poor, marginalized, and forgotten. Health services are few and far between for most children in the world.

My wife, Linda, and I agonize over whether our girls' school system, their teachers, and the corresponding curricula are our best options for nurturing them to be lifelong learners. Meanwhile, over one billion children have *no* options, *no* access to schools; and the majority of schools that do exist in the world are poorly run and costly to attend.

Perspective. That's what we're after in this journey together—perspective. Open your eyes. Wider. Look around you. There have never been this many people alive in the world. Four more babies were just born, and four more . . .

Snapshot 2: Poverty vs. Wealth

Many of our fellow citizens around the globe live in desperate conditions. I continually try to bring this perspective to my girls. The other night, no more than an hour after dinner, Grace, my six-year-old daughter, said, "Dad, I'm hungry. I need a snack." Emily, her older sister, smirked at me, knowing this was the perfect opportunity for my soapbox speech. Right on cue I started in. "Gracie, how can you be hungry? We just finished a good dinner. Millions of children in the world won't get a meal like that all month—"

"Sorry, Daddy," Grace interrupted, "I mean, I *want* a snack."

This has become standing practice for us as a family. Whenever one of us says, "I need . . ." someone else chimes in and says, "Need or want?" My girls love it when they catch me saying, "I *need* coffee." We're working hard to remember that we're among the "haves" when so many in the world are among the "have nots." The chasm between the rich and the poor continues to grow to staggering proportions. Read these statistics slowly and deliberately:

- Twenty percent of the world live on one dollar a day.
- Another 20 percent live on two dollars a day.
- Twenty percent of us live on more than seventy dollars a day.
- The remaining 40 percent are somewhere in between. [3]

And how about this? The combined income of the 447 wealthiest people in the world is more money than the combined income of 50 percent of the world's population. Did you catch that?—447 people have more money than the combined assets of 3.25 billion people in the world![4]

Sisay, a character in Richard Dooling's riveting novel *White Man's Grave*, is an American who has moved to Sierra Leone, where he has become fully immersed as a local. After five years away from the United States, Sisay describes the sickening experience he had going back for a brief visit to the United States:

> I resolved to sit on my mother's front porch and soak up some American village life to remind myself of what I had left behind. It was Saturday. My mother's next-door neighbor, a well-groomed, weight-gifted, vertically challenged accountant named Dave, brought out a leaf blower, a lawn mower, a leaf grinder, a mulcher, an edger, and a weed trimmer. He worked all day, making a terrific racket, chopping, trimming, and spraying toxins on a small patch of ground, which produced absolutely no food, only grass. *The rest of the world spent the day standing in swamp water trying to grow a few mouthfuls of rice, while Dave sat on his porch with a cold beer admiring his chemical lawn.* Sickening? You bet. It was time to go back to Africa.[5]

This is more than creative novel writing; this is reality. Americans make up 5 percent of the world, but we consume 50 percent of the world's resources. Think about that. We consume half the world's resources. The problem of hunger in the world is *not* the earth's ability to produce food for 6.5 billion people; it's the inequitable distribution of food.

Ravi, a seven-year-old boy I met earlier this year in Delhi, is among the 95 percent of the world who aren't Americans. Ravi works ten to twelve hours a day, seven days a week, shining shoes on the streets of Delhi. Ravi faces four years of bonded labor in order to pay back a thirty-five-dollar loan his parents took out for his sister's wedding. Ravi will spend the next four years paying off a debt that's less than what I spent on dinner out last night. The inequities continue:

- More than two billion children live in our world, half in poverty.
- One of every four children in the world has to work instead of going to school.
- Eight percent of people in the world own a car.

Perspective. Perspective on "need." Perspective on "hunger." Perspective on "money." Do you feel as if you're living paycheck to paycheck? You may well be, and my point is not to diminish the financial challenges facing many Americans. But it's all about perspective. It's about serving with eyes wide open.

Snapshot 3: Disease

If that's not enough to ruin your appetite, how about this? Thirty thousand people will die today from preventable diseases. More than three thousand Americans lost their lives on September 11, 2001. We all remember where we were when we first heard the news that day. Three thousand lives were lost in a matter of hours. We pause each year on September 11 to remember the victims and their families, and we should.

Yet how many of us will remember where we were today when we were reminded that thirty thousand people will die *today* from preventable diseases? It's all too easy to read that, say, "Wow! That's horrible," and move on. Thirty thousand people will die today. More than two hundred thousand, the population of the city where I live, will die this week from preventable diseases.

A great many of the lives lost today will occur because the victims can't get basic medicines that I can buy over the counter at a local drug store. Many of today's deaths will be children. In fact, a child dies of hunger every sixteen seconds. Just about every time I take a breath, another child has died of hunger.

- Forty percent of the world lacks basic sanitation facilities.
- Over one billion people have unsafe drinking water.[6]

Perspective. Perspective on the world in which we live. That's where we're headed with all this.

The worst disease facing us is HIV/AIDS. AIDS threatens the social well-being of entire nations. Almost forty million people are infected with the virus, with another hundred thousand infected daily. These numbers are expected to double by 2010.

We must dispel the notion that AIDS is simply a just punishment upon those who disobey God. The number-one way children in Mozambique contract the HIV virus is not through illicit sex but by sharpening their pencils with their fathers' razor blades.[7]

In places like Uganda, the pastorate has become a "burial business." Pastors bury AIDS victims daily, while teenagers and grandparents figure out how to lead households where both parents have died. Over fifteen million children under the age of fifteen have lost one or both parents to AIDS, and that figure is expected to double by the year 2010.[8]

HIV/AIDS has been raging in Africa for more than twenty years. Meanwhile most people, and most churches, have gone about their lives. The next wave of the pandemic is expected to be in India, China, and Russia, home to almost one-third of the world's population. We are at the *beginning* of this crisis, not the end. This is a century-long struggle.

Of the 6.5 billion people in the world, 40 percent live on two dollars or less a day. AIDS is eliminating entire generations in some communities. I know all the numbers can become overwhelming—even numbing—but we must gain perspective on the world in which we live. Let's open our eyes.

Snapshot 4: Displaced Peoples

Too many people on our planet are being forced out of their homes and communities. These people are called *displaced peoples* or *refugees*. There's been a dramatic increase in the number of refugees over the last thirty years. In 1975, 2.5 million people were known to be refugees. Today more than 12 million people have been forced out of their native countries. Another 24 million people have fled conflict and persecution and are internally displaced within their own countries. The vast majority of refugees are women and children, and more than 65 percent are Muslim.[9]

As if being displaced from their homes and communities isn't enough, militia groups, rebels, and government leaders often take advantage of vulnerable refugees. Aid sent to refugees is often intercepted and horded by abusive leaders. Drugs intended to heal children are taken and sold, and food sent to families is enjoyed by warlords. Worst of all, refugees are abused physically and often killed simply to make a statement to other groups struggling for power.[10]

Sadly, young mothers such as Isatu Turay in Sierra Leone are not an anomaly in the twenty-first century. Isatu and her husband were living in a refugee camp in Sierra Leone along with their four young children. One morning heavily armed men entered their house and demanded all their possessions. The rebels became upset when Isatu and her husband had only thirty thousand *leones* (local currency) to give them. On the spot the rebels killed Isatu's younger sister who was also living there and brutally murdered Isatu's husband right before her eyes.

Isatu gathered her children and fled from the refugee camp into the bush, where she ran into another group of rebels who were lining people up and chopping off their hands. Isatu says, "I was praying heavily, and then my two-year-old daughter started to cry. They said the child was causing lots of noise for them. One of them took her from me while another dug a hole to bury her alive. I could not do anything, and my baby cried until she died."[11]

Isatu's story speaks for itself. *Perspective.*

Snapshot 5: McWorld

Globalization is a broad term with many meanings, but increasingly it's associated with the expansion of business and capitalism across national borders. We definitely need perspective on this reality of our world. Marketing products and services that have been profitable in the United States and selling them overseas has often been referred to as the McDonaldization of the world, or McWorld for short.

Like its name, McDonald's is the epitome of McWorld. You can get the same french fries in Quito, Delhi, and Toronto. The most universal product in the world is Coca-Cola. Or consider one of my addictions—Starbucks! You could be dropped into a Starbucks in Bangkok and have a hard time knowing whether you're in Bangkok, Seattle, Shanghai, or Sydney. The same drinks are available; the same font adorns the signage; and the chairs, lighting, color on the walls, and music are all strangely familiar. It's all part of the McWorld experience of Starbucks.

When I travel, I love to eat in local establishments, and I thoroughly enjoy trying new foods. I have to admit, however, sometimes I'm really happy to find a Starbucks where I can get my predictable, favorite drink. Yet I'm haunted by considering the implications of getting Indonesians to switch from tea to Frappuccinos, from sandals to Nikes, from oxen to SUVs, and from indigenous movies to Hollywood. This tension needs to be incorporated into our widened perspective on the twenty-first-century world.

There's a growing movement among American Christian businesspeople called "business as mission." I'm excited about business professionals looking holistically at how to engage in global mission. The people involved in this conversation can help us consider the impact of a global market upon the lives of people living in our own neighborhoods and in communities scattered across the world. McWorld is changing the job market for your friends and mine, and it's changing entire lifestyles of people around the globe. This reality needs to be included in our widened perspective.

Three hundred megacorporations control most of the capital in the world. Nike's holdings exceed those of most national economies in the world, with virtually no controls over their practices. That's just one example. On average, American companies make a 42 percent return on their China operations. Apparel workers in the United States make $9.56 an hour. In El Salvador apparel workers make $1.65. In China they make between 68 and 88 cents.[12] Christian businesspeople need to help us grapple with these realities to consider the ethical issues involved and the accountability structures needed for individuals and organizations working cross-culturally.

Globalization isn't going away; it will keep growing, but we must wrestle with its implications. Look at the scope of GE, the largest corporation in the world. When I think of GE, I usually think of household appliances or lightbulbs. But GE's business is far more expansive—GE is the world's largest supplier of technology to the energy industry. They sell insurance; financial services; medical technology; engine supplies for planes, trains, and automobiles; and a whole range of things I don't begin to understand, such as thermoplastics, fuzed quartz materials, and silicon-based products. GE also owns one of the world's leading media and entertainment companies—NBC. And this is only scratching the surface of the scope of GE's services. We're far more dependent upon GE than any of us realize—from product parts we use all day long, to the energy used to operate our machine-dependent lives, to the planes and trains by which we travel, and the TV programs we watch.

Though GE is the biggest McWorld enterprise, it is only one example of the "big three hundred" that control most of the money in the world. Wal-Mart, Nike, McDonald's, and GE are among the biggest, but even the smallest start-up companies have the opportunity to be global. With a computer and Internet access, one can start a global business almost instantly. The race of globalization won't slow down anytime soon. Open your eyes to the realities of McWorld.

McWorld is creating a virtual, global culture of sorts, especially among youth. A few years ago, a New York City–based ad agency videotaped rooms of teenagers in twenty-five different countries. The convergence of what was found in rooms from Los Angeles to Mexico City to Tokyo made it difficult to see any cultural differences. Basketballs sat next to soccer balls, and closets overflowed with an international, unisex uniform—baggy Levis or Diesel jeans, NBA jackets, and rugged shoes from Timberland or Dr. Martens. "In a world divided by trade wars and tribalism, teenagers, of all people, are the new unifying force. From the steamy playgrounds of Los Angeles to the stately boulevards of Singapore, kids show amazing similarities in taste, language, and attitude. . . . Propelled by mighty couriers like MTV, trends spread with sorceress speed. . . . Teens almost everywhere buy a common gallery of products: Reebok sports shoes, Procter & Gamble Cover Girl makeup, Sega and Nintendo video games, Pepsi, etc."[13]

However, we must not too quickly assume that globalization implies that we're moving toward a uniform, global culture. Cultural differences abound, and we'll see that throughout this book. However, to a certain degree, globalization clearly is shaping the lives of individuals from the urban centers of Shanghai to the remote villages of Madagascar.

McWorld has brought cross-cultural encounters into our daily lives. Working alongside refugees from Bosnia and Sudan, instant messaging people with similar interests across all twenty-four time zones, and working in organizations that assume a global presence are just a few ways we encounter globalization.

Snapshot 6: Fundamentalism vs. Pluralism

While seemingly more philosophical, this last snapshot is as important to our perspective on the world as the others. On one hand, we have a growing movement of fundamentalists who declare, "There is *one* right way to view the world, and it's our way." Simultaneously a growing movement of pluralists declares, "There's *no* one right way to view the world. Discover your own."

The clash of fundamentalism and pluralism is at the center of most contemporary conflicts and wars facing us today. A world coming together culturally and commercially also is becoming more and more divided religiously and ethnically. In the 1990s, words like *jihad* and *al-Qaeda* were unfamiliar to most Americans. Now they're part of our everyday vocabulary. Watching news reports of fourteen-year-old boys in Afghanistan skipping along with AK-47s strapped over their shoulders has almost become ho-hum to us. Yet many Americans are still confused by why the terrorists hate us so much. In relation to suicide bombers, we ask, "What's wrong with those people, that they'd kill themselves in order to dominate innocent people?"

If anyone should understand the conviction and passion driving the terrorist movements around the world, it's evangelical Christians. Jihad, in its mildest form, is a kind of Islamic zeal committed to proselytizing the world no matter what it takes. Of course, it becomes more extreme when it gets expressed through bloody holy war on behalf of religious conviction—just as the Crusades were a case of "Christian evangelism gone bad." As a concept, however, jihad is as familiar to Christians, Hindus, Arabs, and Germans as it is to Muslims.[14] Jihad, an Islamic expression of fundamentalism, is simply the absolute confidence in the truth of one's position.

In contrast, pluralism attempts to eliminate the dominance of any one religion or viewpoint. It assumes that multiple and conflicting opinions and philosophies should exist, and further, should be regarded as equals. This kind of pluralistic philosophy permeates the story lines of movies, songs, and books distributed through globalization. Globalization is typically seen as an expression and agent of pluralism. Yet globalization also seems to be based upon an essential value held by radical fundamentalists—the core value of *domination*. Bringing the world a uniform offering of products, services, and entertainment options is assumed to be good for all.

The coexistence of passionate pluralists with ruthless fundamentalists will continue to create tension worthy of our attention. Such tension is faced by the worldwide community of Christians as well. Lamin Sanneh, a Gambian Christian scholar, says, "Northern, liberal Christianity has become a 'do-as-you-please' religion, deeply accommodated to the post-Christian values of the secular northlands. The new Christianity of the global south and east [e.g., Africa, Latin America, India], which bears the scars of hardship and persecution, will clash increasingly with its urbane and worldly northern counterpart."[15] We'll further explore the realities of the Christian church in the twenty-first century in the next chapter.

Concluding Thoughts

These snapshots are just a start in helping us open our eyes. The statistics, inequities, and sheer enormity of global issues facing our generation can be mind-numbing. What can I possibly do about the fact that 1 in 3,700 American women die in childbirth, whereas 1 in 16 sub-Saharan African women die in childbirth?

I don't want to take us on an endless guilt trip, but I want to bring perspective. Hopefully, these snapshots have begun to open our eyes to the twenty-first-century world. This is just the beginning of widening our perspective. While simply gaining perspective might seem too insignificant a response to these kinds of life-and-death issues, a widened perspective is full of potential for fueling the worldwide revolution God continues to manifest through his church. Hang in there.

One Church

The Changing Face of Christianity

Picture the typical Christian. Who do you see? Perhaps you think of the people in your small group Bible study or the people you pass as you walk into church. Or maybe you think of the groupies who seem to attend every Christian conference and concert that hits town or the elderly woman who religiously reads her Bible and prays each morning. While clearly part of the body of Christ, none of them are even close to the "majority."

The "typical" Christian in the world is a woman living in a village in Nigeria or in a Brazilian *flavella*. The vast majority of Christians are young, nonwhite, poor, theologically conservative, and female.[1] As we grow in our understanding of the changing face of Christianity, there's great potential for improving how we do short-term missions. The Western church is no longer the trendsetter and center of Christianity, though we still have a significant role. Serving with eyes wide open includes changing our assumptions about the worldwide church of Jesus Christ and our part therein.

By sheer majority alone, the Western church *used* to be the trendsetter for the rest of the Christian church. In 1800 only 1 percent of Christians are thought to have lived outside North America and Western Europe. In 1900 10 percent of all Christians lived outside North America and Western Europe. By 2000 more than two-thirds of the Christian church lived outside North America and Western Europe. The center of gravity in the body of Christ has shifted southward. The largest Christian communities today are not in the U.S. Bible Belt but in Africa and Latin America.[2]

As a reflection of this reality, from here on, we'll use the term "majority world church" to refer to the church outside North America and Western Europe. This term was coined by church leaders gathered from these nations at the 2004 Lausanne Committee for World Evangelism in Pattaya, Thailand. They collaboratively rejected the degrading terms previously used to describe them, most frequently "the third world church."[3] Instead, "majority world church" is a descriptive term that refers to the church in those regions of the world where the greatest population of Christians live—outside North America and Western Europe.

Just as with the world at large, it's impossible to accurately generalize about the majority world church. However, since many of us have limited experience with anything other than the churches we attend week after week, it's helpful to pause and consider some of the common threads among the majority world church by looking at a few more snapshots.

Snapshot 1: Unprecedented Growth

Contemporary sociologists are confounded by the pace at which Christianity is growing around the world. Endless predictions were made throughout the twentieth century that suggested Christianity would unravel alongside colonialism. However, "instead of Christianity fading away along with the empire, it unexpectedly grew and spread."[4] New faith communities came into being without a colonial order to maintain them and they grew with a different flavor and look from that brought to them by the imperialists.

The pace at which the majority church is growing is phenomenal. Consider a few of the statistics:

- On average, 178,000 people are converted to Christianity daily.
- Daily, 35,000 conversions occur in Latin America. There were 50,000 believers reported in Latin America in 1900. By 1980 there were more than 20 million and the number is now over 480 million.
- Daily, 28,000 conversions occur in China. When China became closed to missionaries in 1950, there were reportedly a million Christians in China. Today's estimates are nearing 100 million.
- In Indonesia, the largest Islamic country in the world, at least a million people convert to Christianity each year.
- India has more than 85 million believers. Two hundred teams travel the nation with an Indian version of the *Jesus* film, entitled *The Man of Peace*, and report 100,000 conversions monthly!
- In 1900, Korea was deemed impossible to penetrate with the gospel. Today, South Korea is reported to be more than 40 percent Christian, with more than 7,000 Christian churches in Seoul alone.
- More people have come to know the Lord in Iran in the past ten years than in the previous thousand years combined! Thriving churches are found in almost every Iranian city and village.
- Daily, 20,000 conversions occur in Africa. Forty percent of Africa is said to be "Christian" now.
- None of the fifty largest churches in the world are found in North America. Check out the size of a few of these congregations. In Seoul, Korea, there are 253,000 members in Yoido Full Gospel Church. In Abidjan, Ivory Coast, there are 150,000 members in one congregation. Another 150,000 members attend Yotabeche Methodist Church in Santiago, Chile, and 120,000 members attend Deeper Life Bible Church in Lagos, Nigeria.[5]

Some of these statistics may be questionable, so an understanding of what is meant by "conversions" is needed. Simply counting the number of people who say a prayer or espouse to follow Jesus is not enough. We're called to make disciples, who in turn have a transformational impact upon their communities. Regardless, something is happening in God's people around the world. Clearly the revolution of Jesus Christ continues to transcend the many atrocities and inequities described in chapter 1.

Christianity is the fastest-growing religion in the world, with a 6.9 percent growth rate, compared to 2.7 percent for Muslims, 2.2 percent for Hindus, and 1.7 percent for Buddhists.[6] The story of Christianity represents a fundamental and historical shift in worldwide religions. Christianity is not held captive by any particular culture. In fact, more languages and cultural expressions are used in Christian liturgy, devotion, worship, and prayer than in any other religion.[7]

Add the burgeoning growth of the church to your perspective on the twenty-first-century church. Open your eyes. For those of us who are members of God's people, we're part of a worldwide revolution that is growing with racing speed.

Snapshot 2: Persecution? Of Course!

The phenomenal growth of the church has not come without a cost. More Christians have been martyred for their faith in this century than in the previous nineteen centuries combined. Christians in the majority world church suffer brutal persecution. For most of the majority world church, persecution is commonplace and expected. As a result, many portions of the Bible make much more immediate sense to them. The stories of Mordecai, Daniel and friends, and Paul and Silas read like their daily news.[8]

Persecution is especially prevalent for Christians living in the remnant Communist countries, including China, North Korea, Vietnam, Cuba, and Laos. North Korea has been in "first place" for three years in a row as the least religiously freed nation in the world. Religious persecution is also prevalent in parts of the Islamic world, such as Sudan, Saudi Arabia, Iran, Pakistan,

Egypt, Indonesia, and Uzbekistan. These states live by their fundamentalist conviction that there is one right way to see the world—Islam.

You won't often hear these stories in the mainstream media, or even from the persecuted themselves, because for them persecution is just a fact of life when you're a Christian. Almost daily, young Christian boys are stolen from their parents in Sudan and taken to "cultural cleansing camps" where they are forcibly converted to Islam. They're then sold at open-air slave markets. This is happening today! Right now our fellow members in the Christian church are experiencing this kind of Paul-like persecution.

Take a minute and visit Voice of the Martyr's website, http://www.persecution.com/ for a timely story of someone in the majority world church experiencing persecution today.

Snapshot 3: Communal Decision Making

Another reality in the majority world church is their emphasis upon decision making through a community of people rather than individuals. I'm often involved in developing ministry partnerships between different organizations. When I do so with organizations led by American ministry leaders, the process typically involves a few conversations with the key decision makers at the table, and we develop an agreement. Sometimes these leaders include various team members in the decision-making process but at the end of the day, the partnership is solidified between one or two key leaders.

The process is very different when I develop partnerships with ministries led by majority world church leaders. One of the reasons for this difference is their commitment to communal decision making. Majority world church leaders tend to deliberate by thinking about how the decision will affect lots of different groups. This doesn't mean decision making and leadership are approached in an egalitarian manner where everyone has equal voice. In fact, many majority world church leaders are far more hierarchical and paternalistic than the egalitarian style I prefer. However, the decision-making process occurs collectively with lots of different people rather than with a couple key leaders making decisions in isolation.

Historian Peter Brown sees the communal nature of the majority world church as strangely reminiscent of the Christian church in the third and fourth centuries. A radical sense of community is what made Christianity so appealing to people at that time. It allowed people to drop from the wide impersonal world into a miniature community. In the same way, many Christians in the majority world today find a far greater sense of identity with their local churches than they do with being citizens of Peru or Nigeria. Communities of faith fill the void of disintegrated families and tribes, which have been eroded by ethnic cleansing, disease, and famine. The intimacy experienced among Christian faith communities in the majority world is comparable to the intimacy of a large family gathering.[9]

Emphasis upon community and interdependence is one way majority world pastors have adapted the tools and philosophies they received from Western missionaries. For example, the emphasis on helping a church become self-supporting has been a driving agenda of Western missions over the last several decades, as expressed in the "three-self" formula. According to the three-self theory, national churches should be self-propagating, self-supporting, and self-governing. Three-self is an appropriate reaction against "spoon-feeding," where nationals remain dependent upon Western missionaries and Western funds.[10]

However, some majority world church leaders aren't convinced three-self is the right approach. They contend the three-self movement comes from an individualist perspective rather than one developed for an interdependent church around the world. Isaac Mwase, a Christian scholar with roots in both Jamaica and Zimbabwe says, "Unless the economies of poverty in the global South change dramatically in the future, Christian solidarity would seem to demand external support. What is needed is *not* self-sufficiency among the poor, but a way of partnering across cultural and economic differences that affirms Christian solidarity, the interdependency of the Body of Christ."[11]

When 40 percent of the world earns less than two dollars a day and Americans earn more than seventy dollars a day, can there ever be a point where majority world churches support themselves exclusively? These are the kinds of issues we need to explore with the majority world church.

The majority world church believes in interdependence and is trying to teach the Western church about it. We must figure out how to have healthy and mutually rewarding interdependent relationships. This plays directly into how we approach our short-term mission efforts. Our mission trips usually assume we have something to offer the churches and communities we visit, and sometimes we do. However, we must go beyond mere lip service of saying we need to learn from their churches as well. In truth, there is much for us to learn from the majority world church. These snapshots are simply an attempt to help us see a few of the inspiring threads that characterize the majority world church. We'll look more specifically at the implications of these snapshots for short-term missions, but initially let's open our eyes to see the big picture.

Snapshot 4: Beware the "Powers"

Another key thread in the majority world church is their core belief that we live in a dynamic, spiritual universe. While demonic forces are the makings of thriller movies for many of us, principalities and powers are realities to most of our fellow followers of Jesus. Much like the first-century believers in Ephesus and Colossae, people in the majority world have an extraordinary fear of hostile, supernatural powers.

The African church is especially aware of the supernatural world. Africans, whether Christian or not, believe the universe is inhabited by the devil and a host of spiritual forces. Nearly all African religions believe strongly in the existence of all kinds of evil spirits, and that these spirits influence human life in many ways. "Witchcraft beliefs remain pervasive and persistent, and no amount of denial can shift that reality, at least in Christian Africa."[12]

The belief of the majority world church in supernatural and demonic powers doesn't lead these Christians to hopeless fatalism. Instead majority world Christians are much more aware of the importance of being vigilant against the active, dangerous spirit world lurking around them. When asked if they think there's a demon behind every bush, they reply, "There are lots more demons than that!"

The reality of the demonic world to people in the majority world church helps explain their particular interest in Paul's letters to the Ephesians and Colossians. First-century Ephesus and Colossae cultures were inundated with sorcery, magic, and divination. This reality is demonstrated by Paul's frequent references to the "powers of darkness." There are more references to principalities and powers in Ephesians and Colossians than in any other books of the Bible. Many Western commentators have explained away Paul's multiple references to these dark forces as metaphors for the social and political structures that existed in first-century Ephesus and Colossae. Majority world church leaders, however, see these powers as literal, personal, and organized forces of evil with which they must contend on a day-to-day basis. They readily identify with Paul's words.[13]

Most of us as American Christians say we believe in the existence of demons and spiritual forces, but it rarely moves beyond theory for us. We're intrigued by stories about demons when we watch a thriller movie or hear about someone else's experience, yet our day is rarely impacted by the fear of spiritual forces lurking about. This is a key difference in our lives as believers compared to our brothers and sisters in the majority world. This sheds light on the next snapshot too.

Snapshot 5: God's Provision Is Immediate and Direct

Believing in a dynamic universe with supernatural powers all around compels majority world Christians to pray with a sense of urgency and dependency. A member in a majority world church is much more likely to expect immediate and direct provision from God than a "typical" Western believer. You haven't experienced prayer until you've prayed with a group of Christians in the majority world church whose very lives are dependent upon God. Of course, every minute of our lives is dependent upon God as well. However, we have been so influenced by science and the comforts of life in the West that the miracles of Jesus often seem like a first-century phenomenon rather than a reality for today.

In the majority world, huge and growing Christian populations are moving toward the kind of supernaturalism embodied
by Jesus and his first-century followers. This is another reason
why the Bible is more easily understood by non-Western believers. Christian communities in the majority world as diverse as
Protestants, evangelicals, Orthodox, and Catholic proclaim a
Christianity that includes Jesus's power over the evil forces that
inflict calamity and sickness upon the human race.[14]

Obviously many of these snapshots are different angles on
some of the same realities. Belief in the spirit world and day-
to-day persecution are part of why the majority world church
is much more aware of their daily dependence upon God's provision. For example, the belief in God's immediate and direct
provision is often the only coping mechanism available to majority church leaders like Brother Yun. Yun, frequently referred
to as the "heavenly man," is one of China's most persecuted
house church leaders. Yun has suffered endless torture and
imprisonment all throughout his growing ministry in China
while also reporting numerous episodes of God miraculously
sustaining him.

One day after Yun was beaten and paraded through the streets
for several hours, he was brought into an interrogation room
where he was tightly bound, further beaten, and questioned.
Despite Yun's pain and anguish, he experienced an unusual measure of confidence in God's protection over him. "Suddenly I
remembered how the angels had opened the prison gates for
Peter to escape. The rope that bound my arms behind my back
suddenly snapped by itself! I didn't tear the ropes off, but kept
them loosely in place. I decided to try to escape." As the officers
attended to a phone call in the next room, Yun got up, walked
through the middle of the courtyard and leapt over an eight-foot
wall. Yun says, "The God of Peter wonderfully helped me leap
over the wall and escape."[15]

Yun, like most of the majority world church leaders I meet,
prefers not to focus on the many miracles and experiences of
suffering that have inundated his life story. Instead he prefers
to emphasize the character and beauty of Christ. May God
stir us from our complacency through the examples of our
brothers and sisters who believe in God's direct and immediate
provision.

Snapshot 6: Missionaries from Everywhere to Everywhere

Currently Brother Yun is helping lead one of the most exciting missions phenomena in the world—the "Back to Jerusalem"
movement. "Back to Jerusalem" is a missionary movement among
the Christian Chinese church. Don't let the name confuse you.
It doesn't mean they want to rush back to Jerusalem with the
gospel. Their vision is much larger than that. Neither is "Back to
Jerusalem" an end-times approach trying to hurry up the return
of Christ. Rather, "Back to Jerusalem" is what the Chinese church
has titled their call from God to become a missionary-sending
nation. Specifically they believe they have been called by God
to preach the gospel and establish fellowships of believers in all
the countries, cities, towns, and ethnic groups between China
and Jerusalem. Along this route are the three other largest faith
systems—Islam, Buddhism, and Hinduism.[16]

"Back to Jerusalem" is but one of many missionary movements
occurring among the majority world church. Last Friday morning
I had breakfast with a Filipino missionary I'll call Anna. Anna
has been serving in China for five years. I asked, "Anna, how
long did it take you to raise the funds to leave the Philippines
and begin your work in China"?

She replied, "Oh, it was just a few weeks. I found out how
much the airfare was, I told my church, and we began praying.
And a few weeks later I was on the plane."

A bit puzzled, I continued, "But what about the rest of your
support? How about the other funds for your living expenses
once you get there?"

Her face lit up as she said, "Oh, brother Dave, I just live by
faith. God meets my every need."

Or travel to Nigeria. Currently over 3,700 Nigerians are serving as missionaries with a hundred agencies in more than fifty
countries. Nigeria has long been viewed as a mission field, but
now it's becoming a major missionary-sending country. For every
missionary who now enters Nigeria, five Nigerians go out as
missionaries to other fields of service.

Together the United States and the United Kingdom still send
out the largest missions force in the world, but close behind
are India, Korea, and Brazil.[17] We're in a whole new era of missions. We are still an important player and need to continue to

obediently send missionaries from the Western church. But we must realize we're joining missionaries from around the world to go to the world.

Snapshot 7: Help Wanted—Leaders!

Much more can be said about what's occurring in the majority world church, but let's stop with one last snapshot. With the unprecedented growth of Christianity, seven thousand new church leaders are needed daily to care for the growing church. The burgeoning growth of the Christian church is creating a leadership chasm.

- Eighty-five percent of churches in the world are led by men and women who have no formal training in theology or ministry.
- If every Christian training institute in the world operated at 120 percent capacity, less than 10 percent of the unequipped leaders would be trained.
- Eight out of ten nationals who come to the West to receive training never return home.
- Leaders from every non-Western region say their number-one need is leadership training.[18]

We have to be cautious about how we respond to this reality. While leaders say their number-one need is leadership training, many of them don't want to use Western models to meet that need. Many residential training institutes sit empty around the world because they have been ineffective at appropriately providing the leadership training and ministry skills needed by pastors in the majority world church. In addition, majority world church leaders are intolerant of theological training that engages the head and not the heart.

We must also hold the need for leadership training in tension with the knowledge and skills many of these national pastors have acquired through life experience. Brother Yun says house pastors in China have been trained by "the foot chains that bind us and the leather whips that bruise us."[19] Through the seminary of "prison," these leaders have learned many valuable lessons about God that no book or course could ever teach. This "on the job training" coupled with formal training and resources will assist these leaders as they continue to shepherd their congregations.

Ministry training for national pastors is an area where I have a great deal of passion and where I spend most of my vocational energy. This is an area where interdependent models need to be developed to help meet the need for leadership training in the majority world church. A realistic perspective on the realities of the global church has to include the huge need for equipped ministry leaders.

Concluding Thoughts

The shifting of Christianity's center to the south and east in our world is cause for celebration. Sometimes the response to snapshots like these can be one of concern. People in the Western church may ask, "Where have we gone wrong? Why are we suddenly becoming a minority?" I think much in the Western church needs alignment. Yet despite our flawed missions efforts over the last century, God has used these very efforts to expand his church around the world.

Be inspired! God is doing amazing things through his church everywhere. Our brothers and sisters all over the world give us a glimpse into how God is working. They inspire us to remain faithful. The majority world church would want you to know it's far from perfect and has many flaws of its own. That's the beauty of God's amazing ability to take our imperfect efforts and use them to reflect his glory.

I hope you're starting to grow in your perspective of what it looks like to encounter the twenty-first-century world. The world with all its needs and disparities described in chapter 1 is a world where God increasingly calls people to himself. The reality of Revelation 7:9—where people from every nation, tribe, and people group will gather to worship Jesus—has never seemed more plausible. The church exists in some form in every nation of the world. Let us reflect on what it means to be joined together with disciples of Jesus all over the world. Open your eyes to your sister in Egypt and your brother in Chile. We must keep them in view as we do short-term missions.

Conflicting Images

Americans' vs. Nationals' Perspectives on Short-Term Missions

The exciting movement of God among his people all over the world is exactly why short-term missions deserves our careful attention. Never before have more American Christians had the chance to see firsthand what God is doing around the globe. Having used a wide-angle lens to look at the world and the church, now we want to zoom in on our short-term mission efforts.

Throughout the last ten to twenty years, short-term mission trips have become a standing part of most churches' annual calendars. Twenty-nine percent of all American teenagers have participated in some kind of cross-cultural service project before graduating from high school.[1] Physicians, teachers, builders, mechanics, business leaders, families, senior citizens, and youth groups are all part of the short-term mission movement. Many travel as part of teams and some go alone.

Short-term missions has outpaced long-term missions[2] both in personnel and budget. The American church invests more money in short-term missions than in those who move overseas to live as missionaries. However, the vast majority of research and writing in the missions world continues to focus on long-term missions. There is a need for much more scholarly research examining short-term missions. The research included in this section was done as a way to help meet that need. Much of the research came from my own work, both examining the training efforts of American pastors who travel overseas to teach national pastors and studying short-term mission trips among American teenagers.[3] I've also referenced some of the seminal projects that have used sound research methods to describe what's happening in short-term mission trips both for those of us who go and for those who receive us on the other end.

Part 2 is titled Conflicting Images. The reason will be obvious soon enough, but suffice it to say, many perceptions held by Americans about short-term mission efforts are radically different from the perceptions of the majority world church members who host these same teams. I share some hard-hitting data in this section, but my intention is not to shame us or to say that everyone who has done short-term missions has done it wrong. I've given most of my attention to the assumptions behind our perceptions and images as Americans, but plenty could be said and considered about the nationals' perspectives as well.

I've included something as part of the American perspective or nationals' perspective only if it was voiced by enough people to make it a common theme. Alongside national leaders' words of caution about short-term missions, many of them have positive things to say about being on the receiving end of short-term mission teams. I've spent less time emphasizing those, not because I'm trying to make a case against short-term missions but because we aren't lacking for enthusiasm or confidence in the value of short-term missions. Our challenge in the American church lies in putting the passports down for a second to take a closer look at what's going on in short-term missions. I'll tip my hand. I think there *is* a place for short-term missions, but I think many of our short-term mission efforts desperately need to be rethought and reworked.

The conflicting images that keep appearing throughout my research and experiences with short-term missions fall into six broad areas—motivation (chapter 3), urgency (chapter 4), common ground (chapter 5), the Bible (chapter 6), money (chapter 7), and simplicity (chapter 8). Valuable things can be learned from both the Americans' and the nationals' perspectives in all six areas. Much of what follows could be my own biography of things I've done and led others to do throughout my last twenty years of globe-trotting. It's also a chronicle of how my own perspective widened. I pray it will help you do the same. Open your eyes. Look at what you may have previously missed when thinking about short-term missions.

Motivation

"Missions Should Be Fun!"

Through the eyes of Americans . . .	Through the eyes of nationals . . .
This trip isn't a "rough-roach-in-your-bed" kind of experience. We'll be housed in nice clean hotel rooms, eat lots of salsa, and have plenty of time to shop![1]	Thousands of young men and women in China will go as missionaries who are not afraid to die for Jesus. . . . They are not only willing to die for the gospel, they are expecting it.[2]

I love to go to new places and interact with new people. Typically when I travel overseas, I spend most of my day teaching or meeting inside sterile classrooms and offices. So when I get a few minutes to spare, I love to blaze the streets of a new place, to take it all in. Where do the locals eat? Where do they hang out? What makes this place tick? What do people celebrate? What's the history of this city? I think this kind of desire to understand my surroundings has enhanced my ability to learn and serve in other places. At times, however, I'm haunted by a thought: Is my cross-cultural work driven most by my desire to follow Christ or by my sense of adventure?

What makes our short-term mission projects different from another group in town who plans a tour through the same region? When is it mission, when is it "vacation with a purpose," and when is it just "vacation"?

Sociologists have consistently found that the way we anticipate a situation will strongly influence how we engage in it. More specifically, our expectations about a new role or a new environment will directly influence how we experience that new situation, both positively and negatively.

I've tried to incorporate this understanding into the counsel I give newly engaged couples. During premarital counseling, one of my priorities is to align the couple's expectations about marriage with reality. I remember all too well one of the comments Linda and I received while greeting guests at our wedding. A middle-aged woman walked up and said, with an incredibly sarcastic tone, "Well, those were nice, lofty vows. Now let's see if you can actually live up to them!" I waited for her to laugh, but she didn't! At the time I was infuriated. But as I look back on it now, I'm not sure she was trying to rain on our parade. Instead I think she somehow found the need to warn us that marriage isn't purely romantic love songs lived out for forty years. I'm guessing she wanted us to adjust our expectations about marriage away from the romantic bliss of starry-eyed lovers to the realities of two selfish human beings living together for the rest of their lives. Now I don't recommend that kind of wedding etiquette any more than I encourage experienced parents to walk up to expectant mothers and tell them the horror stories of labor and sleepless nights awaiting them. But expectations do shape how we actually encounter new experiences.[3]

What are our expectations about short-term missions and what motivates so many people to participate in them? That's what we'll explore in this chapter. Organizers and mission-trip recruiters play a significant role in shaping our expectations about short-term missions. When observing the benefits cited for why we should consider going or supporting those who go, people give a myriad of reasons. The most common ones are related to the way the trip is sure to change the lives of both those who go and those who receive the goers. We'll look at the life-changing nature of mission trips more in a minute, but first, let's consider a couple other interesting dynamics related to people's motivation for going on short-term mission trips—the "biblical" and adventurous reasons for doing short-term missions.

It's Biblical

The other day I had lunch with a friend who is working hard to get her megachurch engaged in short-term mission projects. She said, "This Sunday I'm making another announcement. This time I'm going for the jugular. I'm going to say something like: 'This isn't just about whether or not you like Mexico or Romania or want to go there. It's a matter of obedience. God has commanded you to go. Short-term missions is about obeying the Great Commission.'"

She's a good friend, so I challenged her. "Wait a second, Debbie! Are you saying people who don't go on short-term mission trips are disobeying God?"

She backed off a little bit, but clearly she sees short-term missions as a matter of biblical obedience.

My friend is in good company. Advocates of short-term missions often look to Scripture to demonstrate the biblical models of short-term missions. Roger Peterson, CEO and founder of STEM International, a short-term sending agency, says short-term missions is the *only* worldwide strategy that exists today to comply with the doctrine of the priesthood of believers—God using everyday people to fulfill his mission. Peterson and his fellow authors then point to more than thirty "proof-text passages" (their words) for short-term missions, which span from the heavenly visitors who came to Abraham in the heat of the day (Genesis 18) to Nehemiah and the short-term construction mission (Nehemiah 2–10) to Jesus and the Samaritan woman at the well (John 4). Peterson is confident that short-term missions has a theological foundation that must not be ignored.[4]

Others have linked short-term missions to a strategy regularly employed by Jesus and Paul. For example, one missionary writes, "[The disciples] had watched [Jesus] sacrifice, serve, love, teach, and heal. They watched the Son of Man deal with popularity and opposition. It was time to send them out on their own short-term trip to copy the ministry that they had experienced."[5]

Does short-term missions violate Scripture? Not at face value, though many of the concerns I'm raising in this book need to be wrestled with in light of what God teaches us about being his physical presence in the world. However, might we need to use caution in too quickly looking back to Scripture to legitimize short-term missions? What was the starting point for the short-term mission movement that has grown to such huge proportions today? Did it come from the conviction of men and women studying God's word and discerning that this was a missing element in the church? Or was it a response to the increased accessibility we have to the world and a way to mobilize everyday people to experience missions firsthand? Clearly we see strands of people doing things itinerantly in lots of different places all throughout God's story, but ramping up into our short-term mission trips based upon the belief that what we're doing is copying what Jesus did might yield some dangerous practices. We'll come back to this in chapter 6 when we examine the misuse of the Bible in short-term missions, but keep it in your peripheral vision now.

It's an Adventure

On the other extreme lies the tension I personally feel as I think about my love for going new places. As I mentioned, I sometimes wonder if my drive to do the things I do cross-culturally is more a reflection of my desire for adventure than it is to truly engage in some more noble endeavor. Is short-term missions simply a way of appeasing wanderlust?

Read the letters and listen to the reports before and after mission trips, and those who go on trips tend to emphasize the so-called spiritual things: the number of souls saved, the lessons learned about prayer and materialism, and the impact made upon the churches visited. However, sit down for coffee with a friend who has just returned from a trip or eavesdrop on the picture party from a returning group, and the adventure of life in a new place seems to be the emphasis. Such conversations are filled with stories about who got stopped going through customs, what it was like to eat the food, bartering the shopkeeper down to a ridiculous price, and experiencing the driving habits of the locals.

Let's be honest. Along with the seemingly more noble reasons for going on a short-term mission trip, many of us love the adventure of it all. It's fun to fill up our passports with international stamps. As participants we try to be subtle about when and how often we ask the group leader about the plans for the "free time" on the trip but we desperately want to know the plans for the "down" times. We're told to make sure our reports back to the congregation focus on the "spiritual" things that happened—not just stories about getting sick and trying to speak the language; but there's an adventure that comes with traveling to a new place. Going to Mexico or Africa is much sexier than going downtown.

Actually some organizations aren't subtle at all about the role of adventure and fun in motivating people to participate in short-term missions. For example, Teen Mania, a youth organization based in Texas, has been taking young people cross-culturally for almost twenty years. Teen Mania reports having sent "43,651 missionaries" on short-term projects called "Global Expeditions." Their recent full-page advertisement in a magazine for youth workers featured this huge headline: "Missions Should Be Fun!" Below it was a picture featuring a group of American youth pushing a really cool-looking canoe down a tropical-like river with a few "natives" in tow.[6]

Teen Mania sends parents, youth leaders, and teenagers an eight-page, four-color brochure explaining all the details of "Global Expeditions." The headline of the brochure reads, "Missions Made Easy!" including a picture below it with an American youth group piled into a jeep that's roaming through high grasses. Turn the page and you see another large photo, this one with six American teenagers standing below an exotic waterfall, looking like they're having the time of their lives.

This adventure-filled, fun-packed motif is often used by local church short-term-mission recruiters as well. Glenn Schwartz, executive director of World Missions Associates, shares the following excerpt from a church bulletin announcement about an upcoming trip to Mexico:

[Our congregation] is sponsoring a women's-only mission trip to beautiful Guadalajara, Mexico! We'll spend the week of June 11–18 in Guadalajara (also known as the shopping capital of Mexico), where we will have the incredible opportunity to minister to, pray for, and teach women in a vibrant church community. And this trip isn't a "rough-roach-in-your-bed" kind of experience either—we'll be housed in nice clean hotel rooms, eat lots of salsa, and have plenty of time to shop! Our hope is to take at least fifteen women (including teenager daughters) on this Mexican Ministry Outreach. . . . We trust that God will expand our hearts for Him as He expands our ministry to the women of Guadalajara. If you're remotely interested in this adventure—or if you're just in the mood for Mexico after all this winter weather—call for more details about this fantastic outreach opportunity.[7]

This fun-filled, adventurous mind-set is quite a contrast from the thousands of young, aspiring missionaries in China who are ready and expecting to die for the gospel during their mission sojourns. In their words, "The Muslim and Buddhist nations can torture us, imprison us, and starve us, but they can do no more than we have already experienced in China. . . . We are not only ready to die for the gospel, we are expecting it."[8]

I really don't see adventure and exploring a new place as an "unspiritual" thing. Having fun is "spiritual" because it's part of how God made us. However, if our driving motivation for engaging in a mission trip is most about the adventure to be had in trekking through new territory, we need to exercise caution. If adventure is most what you're after—go for it. Take a trip there! Explore the culture. Soak it in. Experience it fully. But don't put a "mission trip" label on it. Be "missional" when you go sightseeing in Prague or snorkel in Fiji. Always be looking for ways to call people to follow Jesus. Continually consider how to facilitate peace and justice. But let's beware of taking what ought to be modus operandi for all of us every day as Christians and suddenly calling it a "mission project."

It Will Change Your Life

The biblical calling to engage in mission trips and the subtle (and sometimes blatant) notions of having an adventure-packed experience are part of what motivates many to go on short-term mission trips. However, the top reason people participate in short-term missions is for the life-changing experience it promises them.[9]

Think about your conversations with people after returning from their trips. Or consider your own descriptions of trips you've experienced. What's the most common response to the question, "How was your mission trip?" The response I hear more than any other is "Life changing!" Spiritual growth is the very thing we're promised by many of the people who organize these trips. They say, "This trip will change your life. You'll never view the world or your faith the same way again."

Most people are convinced short-term missions is one of the most effective ways to expose American Christians to the needs of the world. An altered prayer life, a commitment to resist materialism, and a newfound orientation toward servanthood are all ways people describe the life change that occurs through short-term mission projects.[10]

Of the millions of Americans participating in short-term mission projects every year, the majority are teenagers. Twenty-nine percent of American high school students have participated in one of these kinds of trips.[11] Any worthwhile youth group is expected to have a mission trip as part of its annual program. In many cases, there's a six- or seven-year cycle of trips for students to engage in from middle school through high school. Mission trips have replaced the summer camp experience as the standard summer event for most American youth groups.

Parents and leaders who struggle with why we're sending our kids overseas to engage in missions when we aren't doing it right in our own backyards are pacified with the assurance that one leads to the other. Mission trips are said to be the ideal vehicle to help students identify their own culture's consumerist and ethnocentric values, to respond to the needs of the world in ways that are faithful to their beliefs, and to challenge the status quo of how their culture shapes their lives.[12] "Expose kids to the needs of the world," we're told, and they'll be much more engaged in serving their own communities when they come home.

Robert Bland, director of Teen Missions International, is reported as saying, "We tell our people who are leading our teams that we're building kids, not buildings. The purpose isn't just what we'll do for these people, but what these people will do for us. . . . There is not a single purpose in [short-term work] . . . but to us [building our kids] is the first purpose."[13]

The emphasis of using short-term mission trips to change the life of the "missionary" is a drastic change from what we've historically emphasized in missions. Clearly the "goers" have always experienced life change as a result of engaging in missions; however, investing billions of dollars in mission work that is *mostly* focused upon the transformation of the missionary is a radical shift from the missions movement throughout church history. Most mission paradigms throughout the ages have called for long-term sacrifice for the sake of others.[14]

Many argue that while the focus might initially be on the short-term participant more than the "receivers," a long-term vision is required. As short-term participants become engaged in mission, get a view for the world, and personally experience life change, the "receivers" benefit in the long run. Short-term participants are prime candidates for becoming career missionaries. So while the first purpose of short-term missions for people like Bland might be changing American kids, I expect he, as others, would say that in the long term, it will result in changing the lives of people elsewhere.

Meanwhile, a growing number of researchers question the long-term impact of short-term trips upon participants. Some studies demonstrate that while participants come home with lofty aspirations of buying less, praying more, and sharing Christ more, within six to eight weeks, most resort back to all the same assumptions and behaviors they had prior to the trip.[15]

Others are even more critical. David Maclure contends that not only do these trips fail to bring about lasting life change for the participants; worse yet, they actually perpetuate the very things they're intended to counter. Participants come home assuming poor people are doing just fine and are happy that way. Trip-goers come home concluding non-Western countries are backward, given their chaotic road systems and archaic ways of doing construction. "Instead of advancing the cause of mission, the exercise simply reinforces worn stereotypes and old power relations."[16]

So which is it? Do short-term mission trips change our lives when we go or not? Before you jump to your own experiences to defend your answer, let's hold off on trying to answer the question right now. Instead let's pay attention to these dissenting perspectives to open our eyes.

It Will Change Their Lives

The other leading motivation for short-term missions is the chance to make an impact upon the lives and communities of people around the world. Participants are excited about the chance to leave the mundane world of life at home to travel to a different place to share the gospel, build a building, or train a workshop. The kinds of activities in which short-term mission groups engage are pretty diverse. Individuals and teams do everything from medical clinics to evangelistic meetings, drama and musical performances, and building homes and painting churches.

When short-term participants seek financial and prayer support, the benefit upon the recipients is the theme most strongly emphasized. A few of the support letters I've received recently included statements such as the following:

- "Many of the people devastated by the tsunami are not getting the help they need. We have a chance to rebuild the homes of the homeless in Sri Lanka."
- "Most of the Brazilian churches don't have [church] buildings like we do. Our team is excited to build this [Brazilian] congregation a new building where they can meet."
- "We'll be running a vacation Bible school for the children."
- "Ireland is a place without God. Pray for us as we bring the gospel there."
- "This will be the first church building ever built in this city."

These are the kinds of sentiments that permeate the pleas of short-term participants seeking support. These expectations are at the core of students leaving the comforts of suburban America to mix cement for a week in Mexico. These assumptions are part of why giving to short-term missions now exceeds giving to long-term missions.

The assumption that a short-term trip can make a significant impact upon those on the receiving end is an expectation of not only high school students and lay people. More and more North American pastors travel overseas regularly to conduct training workshops. The following comments are typical of what I've heard from North American leaders who participate in these kinds of experiences:

- "I'm excited to equip these leaders [in Columbia] so they can be more effective in their youth ministries. I know how these principles have benefited us so think about the benefit to them!"
- "I'm so excited . . . to take what God's done in our ministry here and multiply it to other places."
- "I would imagine these youth workers have lots of great ideas but do they have a philosophy of ministry? I would guess they don't. I want them to walk away with a good structure for ministry."
- "We have a chance to bring spirit-filled worship to Indonesia. The tiny Christian church there needs the power of prayer released."
- "This is the first time this kind of church-planting training has ever been offered in South India."

These participants wanted to see their own lives changed, but most of all they wanted to change the lives of others. Their mentality is, "We don't do short-term missions for the fun and excitement, or because everyone else is doing it, or because we're told we have to go. *We go to serve and share.*"[17]

While the life-changing impact of these trips upon the nationals is used as a way to motivate people to support the trips, there's been little research conducted to explore whether or not our short-term trips really help the cause of the global church as much as we think. Most of the reports about the positive impact upon local communities come from North American participants and sponsoring organizations, not from those who received the participants.

Those who have researched the impact of short-term missions upon the receivers aren't convinced that these trips are changing the recipients. One missionary says, "Everyone knows that short-term missions benefit the people who come, not the people here."[18] In fact, many missionaries are concerned that the very nature of a short-term trip creates a temporary approach to things that require more long-term solutions.

Kurt VerBeek, a sociologist living in Honduras, is one of the few researchers studying the impact of short-term missions upon the local communities where they serve. One way VerBeek observed this was by studying a North American relief organization's role in helping Hondurans rebuild their homes after Hurricane Mitch in 1998. The organization raised over two million dollars for reconstruction of the 1.5 million homes lost and channeled it through Honduran partners. In turn these partners hired Honduran builders to work with people to rebuild their homes. In addition, the organization mobilized thirty-one short-term teams from the United States and Canada to go down and assist in rebuilding homes. VerBeek was interested in whether there was a greater impact made upon the Honduran communities that received short-term groups as compared to those who received homes built by Honduran builders with North American money.

Through the data collected, VerBeek found no lasting impact, positive or negative, on the Honduran families and communities whose homes were built by North Americans as compared to those who never saw a short-term mission team. In fact, in a moment of candidness, the Hondurans confided that if given the choice, they'd rather see the money raised by each team who traveled to Honduras channeled toward building twenty more homes and employing Hondurans.[19]

Regardless of whether we foster life change in the communities we visit on short-term trips, we need to resist the tendency to overstate the level of impact. Our desire to inspire our friends and family members often leads us to give the impression that what we did was the first, best, biggest, and most effective such effort ever accomplished in this place.

At the very least, the criticisms of researchers should make us cautious in our language. Is God really not in Ireland? Are we really introducing worship to the Indonesian church, one of the fastest-growing churches in the world despite the immense amount of persecution there? Are we teaching South Indians to plant churches, or given the rate of growth in their church-planting movements, should they be teaching us a few things about church planting?

Accuracy or inaccuracy of such statements is not my only concern. In addition: What do these assumptions do to influence how we engage in our short-term endeavors? How do our expectations actually shape the way we come across to national believers who receive us? Failure to step back and serve with eyes wide open causes national leaders to feel as this African leader did after hosting an American pastor who came to train African church leaders for a few days. "He never once asked to see anything that I had done—that just made me feel like nothing we have is worth anything." If our eyes are open to the realities of the majority world church that we considered earlier, it will change the expectations that shape our engagement.

Concluding Thoughts

I'm interested in calling us to consider how our motivation for going on a short-term mission trip influences what happens when we get there. Be encouraged. Honesty about what does and doesn't occur through short-term missions allows us to see our trips as an integral part of our lifelong journey of following Jesus, rather than just a two-week project. As we take our eyes off ourselves and begin to look outward, we see our short-term trips as a way to encounter the missional journeys of local churches in places around the globe.

Opening our eyes to this motivation conflict gives us the chance to revolutionize the way we do short-term missions. We're still on the journey of gaining perspective in order to serve with eyes wide open. We'll revisit this important area of motivation in part 3 as we explore the CQ matrix for serving cross-culturally.

Urgency

"Just Do It!"

Through the eyes of Americans . . .	Through the eyes of nationals . . .
We've got to do something. The window of opportunity is *now*! The time for change is ripe. We must seize this opportunity.	You too quickly get into the action without thinking through the implications on our churches long after you go home.

Time—it's a precious thing. Rarely is a day of my life not carefully planned out. Even my vacation days are twenty-four-hour time blocks to be conquered. After all, planning our family vacation is a way to be sure our family maximizes our "play time" together. I pride myself on getting a lot done in a day's work. I'm obsessed with efficiency. I stand in line and come up with ways things could be done better and quicker. Ah yes, when it comes to time, I'm terminally American.

Seizing the moment and making a difference are compelling forces in our cross-cultural experiences. Clearly this can be a good thing, but just as often our desire to jump in and do something can reflect a human-centered approach to missions rather than a God-centered one. This chapter explores our American tendency to jump into the action and take charge of a situation. We're not known for our reflection or for pausing to think through the long-term consequences of our actions. Let's explore this tendency in us as Americans and as evangelicals and compare that with how Jesus approaches the issue of urgency and time.

The American Way

Think of the number of clichés and proverbs that are part of our everyday vocabulary as Americans. We place huge value on time. We believe it's a scarce, valuable resource. We say:

"Time is money."
"We need to do this sooner, rather than later."
"There's no time like the present."
"Make every minute count."
"It's now or never."
"Haste makes waste."
"The early bird catches the worm."

Our American obsession with time and urgency leads us to want to schedule and control everything. Long gone are the days when kids made the best of playing with the kids next door. We schedule "play dates," we organize "community" with fellow church members in small groups, our lives are so packed we need vacations to get away from home, and even our vacations are often full of one planned event after another. An urgency drives the American way, much of which is embedded with strengths. Our history as a land of pioneering immigrants who rebelled from the Old World has allowed the United States to be a force for much good in the world. We don't merely sit back and talk about how things could be different; we make them different. We take charge of situations and seize the moment.

Movie theatres and hotels greet us with mission statements. Health clubs have strategic plans for how to partner with the medical field in preventive medicine. Churches join other organizations in crafting documents that declare mission, vision, and values, followed by well-defined objectives.

Our obsession with making the most of every opportunity and the entrepreneurial spirit of our American heritage is not without positive impact, but it's also loaded with problems. Our pillaging of Native American land and culture to make a nation for ourselves was deplorable. Our frequent unwillingness to collaborate in a global process that takes more time and effort often results in death—literally! Our drive to make everything happen "now" rather than seeing what unfolds can lead us to be judgmental of people in more laid-back cultures.

Richard Dooling's novel *White Man's Grave* is a riveting story about Michael Killigan, a Peace Corps volunteer who goes missing in West Africa. Michael's best friend Boone leaves Indiana to go to Sierra Leone to look for Michael. With good reason, Boone has a sense of urgency about finding out what's happened to his friend. His urgency goes beyond his immediate mission, however. He applies it to everything he encounters in Sierra Leone. For example, one day Boone observes a little baby who isn't breathing normally, and he says, "I can't stand it. I have to do something." In response to Boone's urgency, his African host says:

> That's when white people are most dangerous. When they try to make things "better" for Africans. When white people are trying to enslave Africans or rob them, the Africans usually know what to do. They've dealt with slave traders, invaders, and plunderers for centuries. They usually quench the world's thirst for slaves by capturing some of their enemies and selling them to slave traders. But when white people come in with a lot of money or "know-how" and try to make things "better," that's when things go to hell. Why can't white people just visit? Why must they always meddle? It's as if you were invited to dinner at someone's house and during your brief visit you insisted on rearranging all the furniture in the house to suit your tastes.[1]

Urgency, taking charge, and making the most of every opportunity—it's part of what it means to be American.

The Evangelical Way

The activist, urgent, "take-charge" ethos of American culture is mirrored in the subculture of American evangelicalism. Pragmatism—doing whatever works in the most efficient way—rules the day in most American churches. Our inspiration and zeal overpower our ability to step back and engage in serious reflection. We struggle with a messiah complex that Jesus himself never had, and he *was* the Messiah!

The question that has dominated much of American evangelicalism over the last several decades is "What works?" Success is measured and defended based upon effectiveness and efficiency. If preaching doesn't draw a crowd, then figure out what will. If the symbol of a cross or reciting creeds hinders someone from coming to church, get rid of them. Business practices based upon urgency and efficiency drive the agendas of many American churches.[2]

A great deal of our evangelical urgency stems from this mindset: "Hurry up and get to work for Jesus! The clock is ticking." Urgency is central to our approaches to missions. For example, the AD 2000 movement has been a significant force in missions throughout the last fifteen years or so. AD 2000 called the global church to embrace the vision to see a church for every people and the gospel for every person by the year 2000. There was an appropriate sense that we needed to work harder to allocate our resources and attention on the people who had yet to hear about Jesus. At times, however, this much-needed attention on the unreached peoples of the world translated into some very human-centered plans of living out God's mission.

The short-term mission movement itself was built upon a sense of urgency. For example, George Verwer, founder of Operation Mobilization, was frustrated by the time it took to mobilize adults from the West to the mission field. He saw the vastness of the need to evangelize and wanted to get at the task now! He was impatient to get on with the work by every means at his disposal.

As Verwer looked around, it seemed the people with the most availability were college students on summer vacation. So he came up with a plan to forgo using traditional missionaries and instead mobilize college students to get at the job. In his mind this was a lot more effective than looking for someone who would have to be uprooted from a job and a house. The short-term mission movement has grown astronomically in the forty years since then.

The very title of one book—*Maximum Impact, Short-Term Mission*—assumes an urgency to what we're doing. The authors write, "For every additional hour required of preparation, for every additional characteristic demanded of recruits, there will be thousands—perhaps millions?—who remain sidelined as too average, too real, too foolish to that particular expression of 'Missio Dei.' In our feeble attempts to birth a missionary without spot or blemish, the world continues to go to hell without Jesus."[3]

The North American pastors I studied demonstrated a strong sense of urgency with their cross-cultural training efforts. One pastor said, "If all the other countries get on board with what we're training . . . we could see the return of Christ much sooner, possibly even this generation." He believed there was so much value to the material being taught that it needed to be embraced by the church globally, and that in turn would result in an earlier return of Jesus. Though most of the pastors studied didn't defend urgency quite that way, nearly all of them did embrace a desire to see measurable results, something that allowed for a laser focus with maximum impact in a short amount of time.

In contrast, here are the kinds of comments I heard as I collected data from our brothers and sisters in the majority world church when they spoke about short-term missions:

- "You too quickly get into the action without thinking through the implications on our churches long after you go home."
- "You come here for two weeks. We're here forever. We're not as panicked about finishing all the projects as soon as you are."
- "You assume we aren't focused because we haven't written up our mission, vision, and values like you have. But we are very clear about what God is doing in our midst."
- "Your strategies and plans are helpful. But where's the Holy Spirit?"

It's hard to be missional without some degree of urgency. But when does our urgency go beyond a helpful, value-added component to what we're doing through short-term missions?

Jesus's Way

When looking at Jesus's way of living life, we find an interesting tension between his ruthless focus on his mission coupled with his ability to take time for the "interruptions." Clearly there was a sense of urgency to how he went about mission, but he didn't seem to talk about it with an overly designed strategy or with a clock ticking in the background. This is evident as far back as his childhood.

By age twelve Jesus was hanging out in the Jerusalem temple talking with the Jewish leaders. The temple was by far the largest religious structure in the world, known widely for its wealth and magnitude. Jerusalem was more like a temple with a city around it than a city with a temple in it. The temple was the center of religious, social, and political activity for people—the epicenter of the entire nation.

So it was a pretty big deal for a twelve-year-old Jewish boy to wax eloquent with the esteemed leaders of Jerusalem. If Jesus operated in the "American way," perhaps his reasoning about his experience in the temple would have gone something like this: "This is a God thing. The window of opportunity is now! It's not every day a young Jewish boy gets an audience with the movers and shakers of Israel. So I need to forgo this carpentry stuff with my dad and leverage this opportunity. There's no time like the present. Carpe diem!"

Yet as far as we know, Jesus spent the next eighteen years secluded with his simple family in lowly Nazareth. Even as the Son of God, Jesus didn't forgo the necessity of preparation that was mainly spent out of the public eye. And though Jesus didn't demand perfection out of those he called to join him in mission, he also didn't seem to be in a hurry to get them to the task at hand.

Jesus also didn't seem to be very "good" at closing the deal with people. He often walked away from people after having left them with a rather nebulous statement. That doesn't seem like efficient "short-term missions," does it? Yet somehow Jesus seemed to believe that the Father was capable of continuing his work in the lives of people long after he "walked away" from them.

Once Jesus embarks on his public ministry, Luke keeps reminding us that Jesus *did* have a destination. Again and again Luke tells us that Jesus was "making his way to Jerusalem." Here are just a few examples:

> Jesus resolutely set out for Jerusalem.
>
> Luke 9:51

> Jesus went through the towns . . . as he made his way to Jerusalem.
>
> Luke 13:22

> Now on his way to Jerusalem . . .
>
> Luke 17:11

> Jesus took the Twelve aside and told them, "We are going up to Jerusalem."
>
> Luke 18:31

> Jesus . . . went on ahead, going up to Jerusalem.
>
> Luke 19:28

Okay, you get the point. Jesus is pretty clear about his destination. He has to get to Jerusalem. The destination of a lifetime awaits him there. So there's clarity about his mission and its urgency. Everything runs through the filter of getting to Jerusalem. But his sense of urgency doesn't prevent him from being compassionate, generous, and spontaneous. Along the way he heals countless numbers of people, he teaches his disciples and crowds who gather to see him, and he doesn't seem hurried or panicked.[4]

What a different picture from how I live. What a contrast to the urgency that seems to drive some of our assumptions about what we must do when we engage in missions cross-culturally.

Concluding Thoughts

The very nature of short-term projects in and of themselves brings a sense of urgency. When we're engaged with a group of people or in a region for only a short amount of time, there's an even greater sense of needing to make the time count. Very typical of the types of comments I've gathered from numerous short-term participants is this one: "We've got to do something. The window of opportunity is *now*! The time for change is ripe. We must seize this opportunity."

A sense of urgency clearly is something we must hold in tension. Value accompanies our urgency. Frankly, I think our ability to help develop plans for our dreams and others' is one of the most value-added things we have to offer the global church, but we must do so carefully. It must happen in ways that are truly shaped by the national church that was there long before we arrived and will be there long after we leave. Most of all, we must not live as if God's mission is somehow contingent upon our plans and strategies. God remains on the throne and continues his redemptive work with or without our frantic sense of urgency.

Common Ground

"They Don't Fly Planes in India When It Rains"

Through the eyes of Americans . . .	Through the eyes of nationals . . .
If there were any surprises for me, it came in how similar everything is to everything back home.	I might look like the kids in your neighborhood on the outside. But what's on the inside is totally different.

I had just finished speaking at a conference in St. Louis. Mike, a twenty-two-year-old Christian college student, was elected to drive me to the airport. It was pouring rain.

"It's a good thing you aren't in India right now," Mike said.

"Why?" I asked.

"Because they don't fly planes in India when it rains," he replied.

"Really?!" I responded. "What makes you say that?"

"Well, I just spent two weeks there. We had a couple domestic flights, and whenever it was raining, they canceled our flights.

I guess they don't have the technology we do for flying in this kind of stuff."

I couldn't decide whether to smile and nod or tell him about the countless times I've taken off from Indian airports in the midst of torrential downpours.

While Mike's naiveté might seem a bit extreme, we have a strong tendency to overgeneralize our unique incidents and encounters cross-culturally in an attempt to find common ground. There are a couple primary ways our desire for common ground gets played out in short-term missions. Our first tendency is to look for the similarities between the new culture and something we've experienced before—usually our home culture or another foreign culture where we've traveled. The other tendency in trying to attain common ground is taking isolated incidents or people and applying what you see in them to everyone in a culture. This is one of the most common pitfalls we make when we encounter a new cultural context.[1]

How are we the same? How are we different? What's an isolated incident or behavior and what's typical of a culture as a whole? We want to face such challenging questions in this chapter as we keep widening our perspective. We'll look at two common ways our search for common ground gets played out: (1) our tendency to look for similarities and (2) our tendency to generalize an isolated event or trait to an entire culture.

People Are People

Eastern or Western, rich or poor, black or white, people are people. Sure, there are differences, but at the end of the day, we as human beings are more alike than different. This prevailing assumption drives the tendency to seek common ground.

More than three-quarters of the short-term participants I've surveyed have commented on the similarities they observed in the new culture with what they experienced at home or in another place. Often this response came from the question, "What surprised you most about your trip?" Here are a few of the responses:

- "Maybe the real point is that they just aren't as different from us as I thought they would be. Or maybe it's that in spite of a few superficial differences, like clothes and food, they are more like us than I thought."

- "I understand more of what is going on than I expected to (not the language of course, but the things people do). I watched people in the restaurant the other night, and there was nothing they did I wouldn't do back home."
- "We're all fallen people, and the issues are much the same because we have the same root to deal with [sin]. I prepared myself for all the differences but I don't think I needed to. We're a lot more alike than different."
- "They struggle with the same things in their churches as we do—elder boards, parents, how to get people to buy into the vision, sacred cows, that kind of stuff. It sounds a whole lot like our church!"
- "The students I taught met most of my expectations. . . . If there were any surprises for me, it came in how similar they and the issues they're dealing with are to the students I teach back home."

Why are we so inclined to find the similarities between us and those we meet in new places? Are our perceptions about our sameness accurate? At face value, there's some real strength to our tendency to find "sameness" in our fellow citizens of the globe. We are all created in the image of God. We all long to love and be loved. We were all created for a mission and to have purpose. We are all born and will all die. Our common bond as humans is evident in crises like the tsunami disaster of December 2004. Suddenly the Islamic-Buddhist-Christian, male-female, East-West barriers were diminished. We watched with horror as our fellow human beings were destroyed by the tsunami. When we begin to see what we have in common with each other as humans rather than being obsessed with the differences, we begin to strip away the "us versus them" mentality.

In fact, looking for common ground with our fellow citizens of the globe is a normal and healthy way of coping with the inevitable dissonance that occurs when we encounter a new culture. Traveling to a new place brings on an irresistible impulse to smooth over the strangeness. We look for similarities because it's reassuring for us to spot something familiar when we go somewhere for the first time. Before we know it, however, we're so focused on the similarities, we fail to marvel at the differences. Only when we've been in a new culture long enough to be repeatedly shocked at the error of our assumptions do we begin to see the things we missed before.[2]

A great deal of research has been done on culture shock, examining the cycles that typically occur for someone encountering a new culture for the first time. Finding common ground is the coping mechanism most often used in the first several weeks in a new place. After a couple months of being immersed in a new culture, the emphasis begins to shift toward seeing all the differences rather than the similarities. However, most short-term participants never go through the paradigm shift experienced by those who move to another context for an extended time period. Short-termers are back to "life as normal" long before they experience the depths of the differences that become apparent after more extended cross-cultural immersions.

The brevity of our cross-cultural experiences ought to alert us about the wrong conclusions we make as a result of the common-ground issue. Indeed many of the behaviors, nonverbal cues, and issues we observe may in fact be familiar. The question lies in whether or not we interpret them correctly. When we're in a cross-cultural context for only a brief amount of time, we interpret everything we see through our own cultural framework rather than learning, over time, to identify with another cultural framework. As a result, the short-term trip has the potential of further reinforcing inaccurate assumptions and interpretations rather than helping alter our inaccurate assumptions. Even multiple short trips to the same place don't necessarily alter them. Continued brief encounters in the same place often result in continued observation of the same similarities rather than exposing the vastly different cultural paradigms at work.

An Indiana youth group who traveled to Ecuador for a couple weeks reported on the consistent joy and contentment evident among their Ecuadorian hosts. In struggling to overcome the language barrier, students found themselves doing a lot of waving and smiling to their Latin hosts; the Ecuadorians reciprocated with equally warm smiles and waves. As a result, the students talked a great deal about the unusual measure of joy and contentment among the Ecuadorian people as a whole. They talked about the amazing love of Ecuadorians for Americans.

Terry Linhart, a researcher and professor of youth ministry, joined this group on their trip to Ecuador as a way to better understand the short-term mission phenomenon. Linhart compares the high school students' interaction with the Ecuadorians to an interactive museum. The students gawked at the "living artifacts" from Ecuador without really encountering them. The Americans worshiped alongside the Ecuadorians, performed for them, and poured out affection on their children. However, with limited ability to cross the chasm of language, the students were unable to make accurate perceptions about the Latins. Linhart writes, "Without spending significant time with the person, visiting his or her home, or even possessing rudimentary knowledge about the person's history, students made quick assessments of their hosts' lives and values."[3] Their reasoning went something like this: "When we smile and show friendliness, that means we're happy. It's a sign of joy. Therefore, these people's wide smiles and aggressive waves clearly prove the contentment and joy of all Ecuadorians."

Those who have studied intercultural communication caution us against too quickly interpreting nonverbal behavior cross-culturally. Smiles and laughter may in fact be a sign of joy, but just as likely may be a response to an awkward situation where words cannot be used due to a language barrier. Likewise a nonverbal response of silence or a lack of nodding one's head in agreement doesn't necessarily mean understanding *isn't* taking place.

I often observe this when black preachers speak to white audiences. Given the ways black congregations often give an abundance of affirming nods and exclamations in response to a preacher, I feel for the black preachers who try to move white, staid congregations. At times, however, I've been among white audiences who have received a tongue-lashing from preachers who assume we're apathetic and disinterested because we don't respond with shouts and nods. The preachers simply engage in the behavior to which we're all inclined—to interpret nonverbal cues in light of how we use them in our culture. The reasoning goes something like this: "When my people are bored and disengaged, they don't say anything. Therefore this white crowd's silence means they're bored and disengaged."

I've often done the same thing when teaching cross-culturally. More than I care to admit, I draw much of my energy when I'm teaching from how the students engage nonverbally and ver- bally with me. I've spent a great deal of time teaching in Asian contexts where both verbal and nonverbal responsiveness tends to be far less than what I experience in American classrooms. Even though I know that, and even though I'm writing about it right now, next week when I'm teaching in Asia, it will continue to be an ongoing challenge for me.

Misreading cross-cultural behavior is one of the most consis- tent findings of my research. The most frequent statement made by the North American pastors I studied was, "These people are so hungry for our training!" Every pastor/trainer said something like the following:

- "They were really hungry [for the training]."
- "The training [was] outstanding. . . . I think they were hun- gry, very hungry. I would even say more hungry overseas than they are here . . . because they're looking for more effective ways and tools."
- "They would sit and listen. They wouldn't get up and go to the bathroom every five minutes or say, "I need a break" every couple hours. They were enduring heat . . . humidity . . . the small environment. . . . And they didn't get up and leave. I mean they were spellbound . . . in listening to the message, the methodology . . . the format . . . the how to's and the philosophy."
- "It was fresh and new [like] they had never heard it before. They really soaked it in."
- "They were so thirsty. They just hung on every word."

I asked the trainers how they came to these conclusions. Responses ranged from "I just sensed it from the questions they asked and from the way they listened so intently" to "I asked them if they were tracking and they said yes." Others drew upon nonverbal feedback, concluding that nodding heads and note taking implied learning was occurring.

In contrast, the most brutally honest student who sat in this training said, "You conclude you're communicating effectively because we're paying attention when we're actually just intrigued by watching your foreign behavior." This national leader wasn't the only one who made a statement challenging the assumptions of the American trainers. Some of the other statements made by the nationals who sat in the training included:

- "It was a nice day, but I don't think what they taught would ever work here. But if it makes them feel like they can help us in ways beyond supporting our ministry financially, we're willing to listen to their ideas."
- "I'm glad the trainers felt respected. They should. What they need to realize, however, is that we would never think about talking or getting up to leave in the middle of their lecture. It would be repulsive to do that to a teacher in our culture."
- "I wish we could have shared more about the real challenges we're facing in our ministry. How do I lead a church when most of our godly men have lost their lives in battle? How do I help a parent care for their AIDS baby? Those are my pressing issues, not growing my church bigger or starting a second service. I didn't get that whole discussion."

While hesitant to be overly critical, more than half of the national pastors studied expressed frustration that North American pastors talked about successful churches in the United States with little awareness of many churches that are far bigger in other parts of the globe. As a result of the tendency to look for common ground, many North American pastors felt the needs among the churches where they were training were the same as those back home. Almost every North American pastor commented on the similarity in the issues in churches cross-culturally. Whether discussing youth ministry, elder boards, getting people to buy into vision, putting people under church discipline, or dealing with expectations of people upon the pastor, most of the North Americans concluded, "Church is church, wherever you go."

Perhaps this explains why one Brazilian pastor described his frustration with what occurred when he attended the training done by a North American as follows:

During our class, I was describing some of the challenges our
church is facing in our Bible study groups. I shared how our
adolescents rarely feel free to speak up because of some dominant
older members. The trainer immediately started to tell me why
this proves our need for a specific program for the young people.
I told him we're resisting that trend because we want to keep
the generations together. He laughed and said, "That's where the
American church was forty years ago, but you're going to have to
develop a strong youth ministry or you'll lose those kids."

Conflicting perspectives between North American trainers and
national pastors were more than occasional. Upon extended study
and review, these two very different perspectives became a consistent theme. North American pastors were operating from the
assumption that "Things here are pretty much the same as home,
so these pastors are really hungry for guidance on how to lead." In
contrast, national pastors said, "You act as if the American church
is the true trendsetter for how we should all do church."

I would be misrepresenting our brothers and sisters from the
majority world church to suggest that nothing of value came from
this training or that it's always a waste of time. Several described
some specific experiences with foreign teachers that really moved
them forward in their lives or ministries. So while you might be
ready to ban anyone suggesting short-term training efforts overseas,
I'm not ready to go there just yet. I am, however, ready to call us
once again to widen our perspective. The point is not that nothing
good ever comes from the trips or the training. Instead my point
is to help us see our tendency to inaccurately interpret what *is* occurring and what's being communicated by familiar behaviors.

One short-term participant said, "I wish I had spent less time
studying the cultural differences because I was really more struck
by the similarities than the differences." On the other hand, a
short-term participant who exercised cultural intelligence perhaps made the most accurate and appropriate statement in relation to this topic: "They are just like us, but not like us at all."

"Everyone" Here Is . . .

When we can't find similarities between ourselves and the
people we encounter in a new place, the other way we seek

common ground is to make generalizations about all events and people in a new place. This is what my chauffeur did when he assumed "Rainy skies in India equals grounded planes."

In Linhart's analysis of the Indiana youth groups' experiences in Ecuador, he reports that all the students on this trip, except one, seemed unaware of the myriad of Ecuadorians who passed each day. These locals seemed to contradict the way the students were interpreting the smiles and waves they received from their hosts. Linhart says the Ecuadorians in general appeared "uninterested in the group, or portrayed facial expressions that were quite different from those who served as the hosts of the group."[4] Even if the high school students accurately perceived the contentment and joy of their hosts, they moved into unfounded territory when they declared that all Ecuadorians are like this.

Linhart is careful to qualify his analysis by saying the students' intentions were honorable and compassionate. Part of the challenge came in the sheer brevity of the experiences, which fostered a near necessity to stereotype—to reduce people to a few, simple, essential characteristics. Fill in the blank: "Italians are all _____." "Indian people are always so _____." "Of course he'll be late, he's _____." On second thought, don't fill in the blanks! Probably several of us would finish those sentences the same way. Stereotypes are ingrained in our perceptions about others. They rely upon us taking a few simple, vivid, memorable characteristics of people we've experienced or heard about in a particular place and making those common to everyone there. We tend to reduce everything about people in a culture to the few, simple stereotypes we have of them.[5]

Some researchers argue that stereotyping can be a positive thing to assist us in cross-cultural engagement. They say that understanding familiar traits and values of a particular culture helps us interact more effectively there. For example, if we understand the way Latins think about time as compared to how we do; or if we think about the communal orientation of most Africans compared to our individualistic drive; or if we consider the respect given to elders in an Asian context—these help move us toward cultural intelligence. The challenge lies in whether such stereotypes are accurate generalizations in the first place.

At best the key lies in holding to stereotypes loosely, and not applying them too quickly to everyone. We must beware of having an experience with one or two individuals from a particular place and suddenly thinking we've now experienced a trait that can be generalized to all or even most people from that place. We ought to resist stereotyping cultures on our own. Some things about me are terminally American. But other things are unique to me and unlike many Americans. The same is true of you. The same is true of the people we encounter when we travel to a new place.

Concluding Thoughts

One day I was at a bus stop in Kuala Lumpur, Malaysia. Standing next to me was an eighteen-year-old Malay guy dressed in an Abercrombie & Fitch sweatshirt, Diesel jeans, and a baseball cap. With his backpack over his shoulder and sipping his Starbucks mocha, he pulled the MP3 headphones from his ears and we began talking. Soon into the conversation he asked me what the kids his age are like in my American neighborhood back home. I started by saying, "Well, you could easily be mistaken for one of them. A lot of them look just like you." He laughed and we continued talking for another fifteen minutes after boarding the same bus. As my new friend got up to exit the bus, he turned to me and said, "Just remember, sir. I might look like the kids in your neighborhood on the outside. But what's on the inside is totally different." If I wasn't convinced before he made the statement, I was then! Our conversation itself was different from what I typically have with teenagers in my neighborhood.

Looking for common ground isn't a bad thing. I actually find it quite inspiring to think about the connection we have with people everywhere. We can find common ground not only with Christians everywhere but with all our fellow image bearers in the world. We share similar fears, loves, and needs. There's something really right about seeing our similarities. But we're wise to discover and embrace the differences between us as well! It's part of serving with eyes wide open.

The Bible

"Just Stick to the Bible and You Can't Go Wrong!"

Through the eyes of Americans . . .	Through the eyes of nationals . . .
We came here to teach about the life of Christ and how he did ministry. And so *cultural differences really don't matter*.	I have never met anyone more insensitive to a local culture, but he said he is transcultural and that he is not American but *biblical* in his values.

I usually get a great deal of empathy, affirming nods, and appropriate gasps for the kinds of things I've shared in the last few chapters—challenging our reasons for engaging in short-term missions, tempering our urgency that can get us into trouble, and questioning what we assume to be "common." However, this next issue—the different perspectives surrounding the Bible—tends to be the one with which people struggle most. Many thoughtful missionaries and leaders have said to me, "I agree wholeheartedly with the things you've been talking about thus far. Our cultural assumptions are dangerous and lead to all kinds of problems. But how can you say that biblical principles aren't cross-cultural? They are!" The mantra that drives most cross-cultural mission work is this: "Methods are many; principles are few. Methods always change, but principles never do."

I realize challenging the mantra that "biblical principles never change" can feel like dangerous territory, but we have to go there if we're serious about widening our perspective for doing short-term missions. The deep-rooted influence of culture goes far beyond the foods we eat, the ways we celebrate holidays, and whether we're chronically "late." Culture shapes the way we think; it alters how and what we learn. Two individuals can receive the same information and their respective cultures can lead them to arrive at two entirely different conclusions.

Culture's influence upon how we interpret Scripture was the issue a group of Western missionaries working in Africa were interested in exploring with some African pastors. They brought in an outside facilitator. The first thing the missionaries and pastors were asked to do was write down what they considered to be the central message of the story of Joseph in Genesis. The shared conclusion of the missionaries was that Joseph was a picture of a man who was loyal to God even to the point of resisting the most intense measure of sexual temptation. The Africans concluded Joseph was a picture of a man who in spite of his brothers' mistreatment, remains intensely loyal to his family.[1] What's the "right" interpretation of this ancient story?

Obviously culture is only one of the many dynamics influencing how we interpret Scripture. Our personality, our family background, our social class, our church experience, and much more all shape how we understand truth. Our purpose, however, is to step back and look at how culture influences the ways we understand and communicate the Bible. We're going to explore different perspectives on the Bible in three different ways—seeing the Bible differently, looking at the danger of "biblical" models, and moving toward a multicultural view of Scripture. It all starts with the question, "What is the Bible?"

Seeing the Bible Differently

I grew up being taught that the Bible was the answer book. We obsessed over values like inerrancy, authority of Scripture, infallibility, objectivity, and absolute and literal interpretation. In our eyes, the Bible was a rulebook with clear-cut categories. We labeled people "liberal" if they didn't land where we did on what was right and what was wrong for all people in all times and in all places. For years I was never struck by the irony of resorting to the authority of extrabiblical words and concepts—such as inerrancy and literal interpretation—to justify our belief in the Bible's ultimate authority.[2]

On the other end of the spectrum were those people we called "liberal," who merely saw the Bible as the story of Israel's experience with some symbolic and allegorical application for today. The miracles weren't to be taken with historical accuracy but rather as images and metaphors to teach us something about life with God.

As I began traveling the world and encountered believers in different places, neither my fundamentalist perspective nor the so-called liberal stance seemed to represent the heartbeat of the Bible. Reducing the Bible to a rulebook or a "manual for the Christian life" didn't seem like a very high view of Scripture. On the other hand, why would I give my life to obey words that were merely symbolic in nature, much less challenge others to do so?

I began to abandon the bibliolatry[3] of my past and see that even the Bible itself was *not* the end but rather a *means* to the end—Jesus! We have to stop worshiping the Bible and get back to worshiping Jesus. Don't lose me here. I'm not saying the Bible is unimportant. In fact, I'm calling for a heightened view of Scripture that sees it for what it is.[4]

In our obsession with making the Bible the end-all rather than a means to the end, we've imported far too much Western culture into understanding the purpose of the Scriptures. Brian McLaren, an author and pastor in Maryland, writes, "We want [the Bible] to be God's encyclopedia, God's rule book, God's answer book, God's scientific text, God's easy-instruction book, God's little book of morals for all occasions. The only people in Jesus's day who would have had anything close to these expectations of the

Bible would have been the scribes and Pharisees."[5] Study the writings of Enlightenment philosophers like Sir Isaac Newton, Rene Descartes, and David Hume and you'll understand the incorporation of concepts like authority, inerrancy, objectivity, literal, and foundationalism into evangelicalism.

Am I saying the Bible isn't true and reliable? Not at all. I'm saying it's far *more* than a "rulebook"! It's the Story of God! It's God's telling of history. It's messy. It includes God drowning most of humanity and killing off Egyptian babies. It calls David—a powerful king who murdered a man and committed adultery—a "man after God's own heart." I don't get a lot of that stuff. But I refuse to rob God's Story of the mystery by neatly explaining it all away. We have to embrace the Story for all it is and be on a lifelong quest to deepen our understanding of it as a way to know and follow Christ.

Part of seeing the Bible differently means moving away from being predominantly interested in what the Bible means for *us* and moving toward a growing interest about what the Bible meant in its *original* context. Only through this kind of rigorous historical work can we move toward a fuller comprehension of what the authors themselves were trying to say. The challenge is, we often reduce the Bible to our subjective interests—"What does it say to me?" We end up making the text say whatever we want it to say, and as a result, we're doomed to having as many interpretations of the text as there are interpreters. Ironically while we espouse commitment to the absolute authority of the Word, we often disregard the original intent and "refashion the text in our own image."[6]

So if the Bible is not mainly a rulebook or manual of Christian living, what is it? It's about God saving his people *from* himself, *for* himself. It's about his agenda in the world to continually advance his glory. It's meant to draw me to the authority of *Jesus* in my life first and foremost. My understanding of the Story is always shaped by my prior assumptions—my culture, my upbringing, my experiences, and more. That doesn't mean the Bible is merely subject to what I want it to be, but it does mean I always see it through my thwarted and limited perspective. However, as I begin to view the Bible most as "story"—the overarching story by which all other stories make sense—it brings perspective, meaning, and hope. We're invited to continue the story of God as the people who have been called by the one true God to be his agents in the world. Our story is "the story of God's redeeming presence as narrated in and through the Scriptures."[7] What a source of identity!

How does our view of Scripture influence our cross-cultural practice? Short-term mission projects often include teaching the Bible in some way. Whether it's communicating the gospel with people on the street, teaching children in vacation Bible schools, preaching in churches, or training a group of leaders, we're often put in places where we refer to the Bible. Seeing the Bible differently doesn't mean we toss using it at all. It simply means we begin to see the assumptions we bring into our reading and teaching of the Bible.

The Danger of "Biblical" Models

We become most susceptible to the downfalls of misusing the Bible cross-culturally when we teach "biblical models." I'm not suggesting that models based upon "successful" churches or from individual personalities are better. Clearly the Bible is a good starting point, but when we make our interpretation of the Bible the almighty trump card by proof-texting our models for ministry, we're in danger of heresy. Ironically, the one who's made to feel like a heretic is often the person who questions whether a ministry strategy is truly "*the* biblical model." We must beware of arrogantly thinking we can organize the global church around some strategy we're convinced is "biblical," when it might be in fact yet another cultural model.

I spent several years working with a training organization that claims, "We teach timeless, transferable principles, therefore our biblical strategy applies worldwide, whatever the context." The problem is, as we sought to implement that biblical strategy in Africa, African leaders insisted on some necessary adjustments to "Jesus's strategy." The same thing happened in India, Brazil, Korea, and the U.K. Many recipients of the training weren't convinced this was the timeless, transferable strategy of Jesus. Was it a helpful framework for ministry? Sure. Did it reflect some of the passions and priorities of Jesus? Definitely! Was it Jesus's strategy? Not really.

One day a North American pastor who trains cross-culturally for this organization said, "Look. The same plan Jesus used two thousand years ago is the same plan we must use today. That's the beauty of our training philosophy. It works everywhere. Don't tell me it doesn't work in your context. You have to make it work. Jesus said so."

This stems from the church's longtime practice of reading the Gospels as if they were given to us so that we could mimic what Jesus did in the first century. John 20:21 often is used as the proof-text for copying Jesus's ministry. "As the Father has sent Me, I am sending you." But to use that isolated verse as fodder to mimic Jesus's ministry one for one is dangerous. Jesus's ministry was geared specifically toward Israel. He came to act out the presence of Yahweh in Israel's very specific story. What God did through Jesus the Messiah was unique and climactic. And so simply reducing Jesus's ministry to a strategy for us runs the risk of reducing the cross to a cute symbol of sacrificial love rather than the moment in history when God defeated the powers of evil and dealt with the sin of the world once and for all.[8]

You might become nervous here and think I'm saying that this somehow means Jesus is irrelevant for us today. I'm not saying that at all! What I *am* saying is that we must grow in our understanding of the historical Jesus within the first-century Palestinian world, so that we can follow Jesus more faithfully in our twenty-first-century world. We have to see more clearly who he was and how he responded to the realities of his cultural context as well as his unique mission.

For example, when we use Jesus as a model for leadership, we have to understand the world in which he led—a world where Rome was in control, Herod reigned, John was beheaded, and Jewish messianic movements were dreamed and schemed—a world where Jesus preached the Good News of the kingdom. There in the dust and drama of ancient Israel I discover the essence of what it means to embody Jesus in the cultural contexts where I lead. The convictions that drove him then and there give me the resources I need to be a faithful follower and leader here and now. However, I can't simply resort to trying to mimic one for one what Jesus did as a leader. Christ developed his ministry priorities in light of his cultural context. He didn't import a ministry strategy from another culture and force it into the first-century world of Palestine. He didn't take principles developed in one place and try to implement them in another.[9]

Others try too hard to set up the early church in Acts as *the* biblical model. Many attempts have been made to offer transcendent blueprints for church based upon what we know of the first-century church. However, the first century took on a variety of "personalities" as it expanded to different cultures and diversity was the norm. For those who wish to get back to the New Testament church, because it was somehow better, there was no single model for the church in the first century.[10] Churches with a Jewish background—such as those in Jerusalem and Antioch—differed considerably from certain churches in the Greco-Roman world such as those in Ephesus, Corinth, and Rome.

Now clearly the New Testament provides us with some directions for how we should go about living *our* part of God's story. Jesus gives us glimpses of what it looks like to live as we were intended to live in a very specific time and place. The early church gives us a tangible picture of what it looks like for God to continue living on earth through his body—the church—in a variety of cultural contexts. But we must not force a strategy developed for another time and place into our contexts, much less another cross-cultural ministry context. Instead we must discover the consistent patterns for ministry that surface throughout the Story of God and find out what those look like in thousands of cultures around the world.[11]

We elevate the Bible when we seek to understand the life experiences and cultural settings of biblical authors and characters. That in turn helps us to discern what it looks like to live out God's presence in different cultural settings today. As we wrestle with the ongoing work of God throughout the world, may we learn about who he is and how he relates to people through the world.

A Multicultural View of the Bible

One of the greatest benefits that comes from traveling to another part of the world is the chance to see the Bible through the eyes of God-fearing people in another culture. Whether Joseph is about loyalty to God despite sexual temptation or loyalty to one's family despite mistreatment is only the beginning of what it means to see a biblical author's intent through a multicultural lens.

The Global God[12] is a collection of essays from evangelical scholars around the world. Each scholar describes the attribute of God that is most evident in their respective cultures. For example, Dieumeme Noelliste of Haiti describes the emphasis that the Afro-Caribbean Christian church places upon the transcendence of God—that is, the infinite ways God is different from us as humans. In contrast, many of our American worship songs emphasize God's immanence—the close, intimate relationship we can have with God and the ways God is like us. Noelliste believes the global church has much to learn from Caribbean believers' understanding of the unspeakable, unfathomable, mysterious holiness of God—God's transcendence.

In contrast, Tsu-Kung Chuang describes the way Chinese people really don't see the point in separating God's character into transcendent and immanent qualities. Chinese thought has always embraced a continuous unity between the supernatural and natural. They look for the "sacred" in the "secular" and the "secular" in the "sacred." As a result, Chinese Christians have little difficulty in embracing a God who is simultaneously like us and unlike us. They don't see much value in the artificial categories of God's transcendence and immanence.

As an American I think transcendence and immanence are extremely helpful ways for me to understand God. I need to embrace the tension of a God who is both from above and right here. However, think of what it would mean for me to dogmatically teach the principles of transcendence and immanence to a group of Chinese believers. The principles aren't necessarily ones they even need and may in fact detract from their cultural understanding of God. In dialogue, however, they can learn from the reasons why I see the need to look at both expressions of God separately, just as I grow from hearing them describe the continuity of the yin and yang of God's character.

The point is not that God is whatever each culture wants to make him to be. Instead our cultural perspectives both limit and enhance our understanding of who God is. My cultural perspective, by itself, gives me a very limited view of the supreme

Creator of the universe. However, as I intersect my growing understanding of God's immanence with my Jamaican sister's growing understanding of his transcendence and with my Chinese brother's growing understanding of the amazing unity within the mysterious person of God, together we have a more accurate picture of God than any of us have apart.

This is why assuming we can simply pick and choose biblical principles to dogmatically share with people cross-culturally is filled with problems. Notice the contrast between these North Americans' perspectives on the "biblical" material they taught cross-culturally and the perspective of the majority world church pastors who received the training. The North American pastors and trainers said:

- "We came here to teach about the life of Christ and how he did ministry. So *cultural differences really don't matter.*"
- "I got really frustrated with [the missionary] today when he kept saying, 'There are many different ways you can approach working with youth.' This is not just one of many good approaches. *This is how Jesus did it.*"
- "At first I was stressed in thinking about 'What does ministry look like here?' . . . Then I took a deep breath and remembered all we're teaching are biblical principles, and as long as we stick to those, they're cross-cultural."
- "It's so cool to think that the principles we're teaching are totally transferable for anywhere in the world. Any church, any ministry. It works. It's biblical."

I sat with the national church leaders who sat under the trainers who made the above statements. After multiple encounters with them and many gracious comments on their part about the trainers, they began to say the following kinds of things in assessing the training they received.

- "In some ways, he described a different Jesus than the one we know. I'm not sure what to do with that."
- "I was surprised we studied Jesus's ministry without really considering any of his miracles and his battling against the supernatural."

- "He kept saying that the primary principle from Jesus's ministry was that he started with a small group and grew a large following. That seems like a very American way of looking at it though. Everything always has to be bigger and better. One of the things we find especially freeing about Jesus's ministry is that it seems his following kept getting smaller and smaller the closer he got to the end."
- "I really enjoyed the materials on how to make our ministry healthy. But why do you think we didn't look at the subject of persecution at all? That seems inconsistent with how God has grown the gospel."
- "I really like the structure. It's good. But I don't think it's the only biblical way to do ministry."
- "I have never met anyone more insensitive to a local culture than this American trainer. . . . I even told him he is terminally offensive in our culture. He said he is transcultural and that he is not American but biblical in his values."

As I've said before, it would be myopic to say there was nothing of value or no truth spoken in what was trained. On the other hand, a realistic perspective will help us pause to look at what is truly biblical in our teaching and what are merely programs and emphases shaped by our cultural contexts. The typical response to conflicting cultural perspectives on the Bible is to try to strip away anything that is cultural, which of course is impossible. Regardless, cross-cultural trainers often attempt to overcome the cultural bias in their teaching by avoiding all use of illustrations. Recipients ask for the opposite. They don't find purely conceptual material devoid of any examples very helpful. Teaching our culturally based models of ministry can be helpful as long as we're careful not to "overbiblicize" them as being the only way to minister.

In addition, there *is* a place for "principles." Principles can express the bullets of a larger assumed story. That's not all bad. In fact, it's essential because we can never give a comprehensive account of how our particular topic connects with the entire story of God. We just need to realize that principles, much as single passages of Scripture, are always inadequate at giving the full narrative. They help provide a structure by which to communicate truth, but we must never contend that they are the best way to express what needs to be done and understood by everyone everywhere.

Concluding Thoughts

A few weeks ago I was presenting this material with a group of leaders when a hand shot up and a pastor started shouting (literally) at me, "How do you argue with the Bible?! If the Bible isn't cross-cultural then we have a more basic problem. We've moved out of the realm of orthodoxy!"

I tried to defuse his rage by suggesting I wasn't interested in arguing with the Bible. I'm interested in questioning who decides which principles of the Bible are truly transcultural and how you extrapolate those principles devoid of culture.

God's redemptive story is unquestionably applicable to every tribe, nation, and tongue. However, our understanding of God's Word is always skewed by our cultural context, and at the very least, our cultural biases need to be acknowledged up front when teaching from the Word at any time, but especially overseas. My perceptions of Jesus are filled with twenty-first-century Western assumptions. I need to grow in gaining a more accurate first-century picture of Jesus so I can do the hard work of understanding how to embody him in the twenty-first century.

Conflicting perspectives on the Bible shouldn't paralyze us from teaching. We must use the Word to help us communicate who Jesus is with passion and conviction. I'm not interested in softening our confession of the Lord Jesus Christ as having absolute authority. But in the midst of our passionate teaching, we must continually recognize the relativity of the cultural forms and language we use to express who Jesus is.[13]

There is only one Jesus and only one Bible that records his words. The difference lies in the prior assumptions we bring to studying Jesus and his Word. We must always leave our perceptions of who he is subject to correction. The Christian message is truly universal in scope. "The truth is becoming ever-more apparent . . . that Jesus is at home nowhere in this world, yet everywhere."[14]

Money

"They're So Happy"

Through the eyes of Americans . . .	Through the eyes of nationals . . .
Listen, we who were born in America have to understand, we hit the lottery by growing up here.[1]	Why do they think we're so poor? What makes them think we want what you have?

A few years ago our family lived in Singapore for several months. After being there for a few weeks, Linda and I decided it was time for our girls to encounter a little broader taste of Asia. We wanted them to taste and see something other than Singapore's slick, modernized streets lined with Starbucks and trendy shopping centers. So we crossed the straits of Johor and entered the world of Malaysia. Customs itself was a whole different world compared to the efficient, high-tech passport control we'd just left in Singapore. Within our first few minutes in the developing world of Malaysia, we were solicited for money, we walked by a leper, and pungent aromas filled the air. I was totally energized. I love robust, raw places like Johor. And I was excited about the chance for our family to get a taste of a place that much more closely resembles where much of the world lives than either Singapore or our neighborhood back home in Midwest America.

Prior to leaving Singapore, we'd told our girls to each pick out a toy they could give a child in Malaysia. We described for them the poverty of many of the children in places like Malaysia. Emily, my oldest daughter, picked out a stuffed frog, and Grace chose some candy to give away. Clearly these weren't "sacrificial gifts," but we were going to start small with instilling in them a spirit of generosity. The girls were excited to embark on a "short-term mission" of their own.

Not too long into our "day in Malaysia," it began to rain. We were stranded under a covered walkway for several minutes. As I looked around me, I saw a Malay man with his daughter. They were just sitting in the dirt and looked like prime targets for our "planned generosity." I leaned over to Emily and said, "See that little girl over there. I bet she would love the frog you brought. Let's go take it to her." Wide-eyed, Emily and I walked over to the little girl, tried to communicate nonverbally a bit, and handed her the stuffed frog. The little girl hugged it and held it close to her. After a few minutes of smiling back and forth, we didn't know what else to do so we smiled and started to walk away. As we started to leave, the Malay father ordered his daughter to return the frog. We motioned that we didn't want it back, but he insisted. He began to raise his voice and grabbed the frog and handed it to me. I tried once more to express that we wanted her to have it, but he wouldn't hear of it.

I walked away, a little frustrated that my daughter's first experience with giving to the developing world wasn't going quite the way I had hoped. We eventually found some kids who took our girls' gifts, but it wasn't nearly as easy to give our stuff away as we thought. As I began to talk with Linda about it, we thought back to our home in the Chicago area. Though a beautiful house, our home was one of the more modest homes in our town. Linda asked, "So how would you feel if one of the parents in the million-dollar homes near us suddenly walked up to our girls and started handing them gifts?" All of a sudden I began to see this in a new light. I thought about how I would feel if some rich person started giving my girls unsolicited gifts in my presence. I'm quite capable of caring for them, thank you!

The last thing I want to imply is that we should keep our things to ourselves in case we might insult people by our generosity. However, I do want to raise the tension that comes from encountering people who live with a very different level of financial resources than we do. Generosity brings with it subtle but important issues of power. We need to widen our perspective to think about how to respond to the poverty we often encounter when we travel to new cultural contexts. We want to explore the "power of generosity" through three questions: Who's "poor"? Who decides what the needs are? and To give or not to give?

Who's "Poor"?

The other night I watched Diane Sawyer's interview with Brad Pitt. My friends were mocking me for telling them they had to make sure they watched this. My alibi was Pitt's involvement in the "One" campaign, (www.one.org), a global campaign to reduce poverty. The mantras of the One campaign are as follows: "*One* billion people live on less than *one* dollar a day. *One* by *one*, we can help them help themselves." I'm glad to join a collective voice that calls each of us to consider what we can do to respond to poverty. The goals are ambitious—to cut global poverty in half by 2015 and to rid the world of extreme poverty by 2025.

Regardless of how you feel about the government getting involved in reducing global poverty, a key emphasis of the One campaign, Pitt's participation in this cause is endearing. He told Sawyer, "I can't get out of the press. These [Africans] can't get in the press. So let's redirect the attention a little bit. It drives me mental seeing what I've seen and knowing that it doesn't show up in our news every day. I mean, literally thousands of people died today!"

Amid his good intentions, however, he kept saying, "Listen, we who were born in America have to understand, we hit the lottery by growing up here, by being born here."[2] Pitt commiserates with those poor Africans who didn't get to be born in the land of the red, white, and blue. I don't want to undermine someone from Hollywood speaking to a good cause. Praise God for that! Frankly, the church could take some cues from people like Pitt who are casting a vision for something so noble. Pitt's lottery-winning sentiment, however, is one of the troubling comments I hear from short-termers as they return from the majority world. We come home talking about how blessed we are to live in America. I don't want to disregard for a second the huge privileges that come our way simply by being Americans. However, are we implying that those not born in America *aren't* blessed? We must resist thinking everyone longs to live here. There are privileges that come with being African and Chinese and Latin. There are blessings inherent to people living in places all over the world. Let's bring perspective to realizing not everyone in the world longingly wishes they had been born American.

Not all Africans are starving and waiting for heroic Westerners to come and save them. People in places like Ethiopia, Ghana, and Uganda are very grateful for the money raised through efforts like the "One" campaign but hate the idea that the world still sees Africa as a place "where nothing ever grows, no rain nor rivers flow" as sung in Bob Geldof's twenty-year-old hit, "Do They Know It's Christmas?" The message of Ethiopia as a starving, helpless country has so permeated our thinking that Ethiopian Airlines offices around the world continually field inquiries from travelers who wonder if they should bring their own meals on an international flight.

While the poverty, illiteracy, and disease throughout Africa is devastating, Africa is also a place where many people are not starving. Democracy has begun to take hold in many of its nations, and Africans currently grapple with answers to their own problems. More than 90 percent of Africans surveyed by a recent BBC pool said they are proud to be African.[3] They don't feel like they lost the lottery!

Short-term mission endeavors often force us to face the issue of poverty head-on. My friend Ashish came from Northern India to visit me in Chicago a few years ago. We were eating at Gino's Pizzeria one day and ran into a youth pastor I knew, along with his youth group. They had just returned from Central America and were spending a day in Chicago to debrief their trip. Ashish asked the group, "So what did you learn from your trip?" Student after student obsessed about the poverty of "those poor people."

After the youth group left, Ashish said to me, "Why do they think we're so poor? What makes them think we want what you have?" Sipping my third refill, I retorted, "Ashish. Give me a break! This is a good thing. Financially speaking you *are* poor compared to any of those kids. It's so hard to get their minds off their consumerist passions. I'm really grateful to hear they experienced some dissonance when they saw the poverty."

Ashish rebutted, "Well, that's nice and all, but I'm so sick of the sympathy of Westerners who think we need more stuff. Why would that have anything to do with our happiness? Please don't help import the idol of consumerism into India." He went on to tell me about the American group who were just with him in Delhi. "They were really concerned about the bicycle I used to get back and forth to church," he said. "They found out how 'inexpensively' they could purchase me a car, and without even asking me, they informed me they had all chipped in to get me a little car! The last thing I wanted was a car. I had to find a tactful way of telling them that if they really wanted to invest in something, I had several members in my church who could use those same dollars to help set up a microenterprise development. But I think I kind of 'rained on their parade' as you say. They thought I was just being supersacrificial."

Granted, some Indians would have jumped at receiving a car from well-intentioned Americans. Some Africans wish they had been born in America. I'm merely trying to get us to slow down a little in our assumptions about the true needs of the world and how we're responding to them. The last thing I want to do is diminish the importance of giving sacrificially and generously. We need to do that; but as with all the other realities we've been encountering on this journey together, meeting the needs of others requires us to question our assumptions before acting. We need to serve with eyes wide open and understand there are ways we're poor and ways we're rich. The same is true in the majority world.

In our attempts to be generous, we presume others want what we have to give them. Worse yet, we are sometimes the first ones to suggest to the majority world that they're poor. One Ugandan church leader said it this way, "We did not know we were poor until someone from the outside told us."[4]

Who Decides What the Needs Are?

One of the things that drove me to write this book was my concern that short-term missions just might continue to operate on the same mistakes that have been true about our mission work in the past. The assumption that we know what is most needed by people in another place is the assumption that allowed Rome, England, and Spain to say their colonialist domination was not purely self-centered. Our financial wealth, and all the amenities that accompany that, easily inclines us to think we know what these people need.

I'm often at national conventions where short-term mission organizations are exhibiting. When I walk up to talk to ministry reps from these organizations, I ask them how the national church is engaged in what they're doing. Consistently I hear, "Oh yes, we're very committed to working with the national churches there. We ask them if they want to be involved." Did you catch that? We ask them if *they* want to be involved. Maybe we should start by asking if *we* should be involved at all, and if so, how? What might it look like if nationals helped us open our eyes to the real needs? Not only is it colonialist to invite nationals' input on the back end of planning, but we often end up doing irrelevant and costly work. Local ownership means more than inviting participation or asking for input. It means letting the local churches actually direct and shape what we do in our cross-cultural efforts; they ask *us* if we want to be involved rather than vice versa.

Building projects are one of the most popular kinds of short-term mission endeavors—building churches, rebuilding homes after a natural disaster, building ministry centers, and so on. I've done my share of mixing cement, painting walls, and nailing in studs. Believe me, if you knew my total ineptness at any kind of "home-improvement project," you'd get a good laugh thinking about me trying to put a roof on a church building in South America.

How do the locals feel about our building pursuits on "their" behalf? As with most of these issues, the reviews are mixed. Many nationals express gratitude for seeing fair-skinned kids give up two weeks of vacation to sweat it out as they mix cement all day long, a world away from their backyard swimming pools. We've all watched the video testimonials about how life is completely different now because of the homes built, the hospital maintenance that took place, and the brand-new roof on the church.

As you would imagine, others struggle with the thought of how many locals could be employed by investing the money spent on a typical short-term building project. Local ministries see short-term groups raise money for a one-week trip that exceeds the national ministries' annual budgets. Jo Ann VanEngen, a missionary in Honduras, contends, "Short-term mission groups almost always do work that could be done (and usually done better) by people of the country they visit. The spring-break group spent their time and money painting and cleaning the orphanage in Honduras. That money could have paid two Honduran painters who desperately needed the work, with enough left over to hire four new teachers, build a new dormitory, and provide each child with new clothes."[5]

One Honduran bricklayer had this to say about his experience working with a building team that came down: "I found out soon enough that I was in the way. The group wanted to do things their way and made me feel like I didn't know what I was doing. I only helped the first day."[6]

Across the ocean in Africa, a leader in Zimbabwe asks us to remember that Africans also know how to build buildings. In talking about one of the groups visiting his community, he says, "It isn't that they didn't work hard. . . . But they must remember that we built buildings before they came, and we will build buildings after they leave. Unfortunately, while they were here, they thought they were the only ones who knew how to build buildings."[7]

Is it wrong to build buildings when we go? Some think so, but I don't. I think there's a place for it, but we must temper such projects with our understanding about the true needs and what we truly have to offer. We *do* have something to offer, but let's discover what that is through dialogue with the majority world church. A group from my church just returned from a couple weeks in Rwanda. Within their first hour in Rwanda, the local team said, "Ninety percent of your job is done. You're here. Your presence speaks volumes." One of the team members told me she thought, "Well, I don't think so. That's gracious of you, but we're here to work hard." The longer she was there, however, the more she began to see that the tasks they came to do were not what was needed most. The presence and chance for relationship together seemed to be the most pressing need for the Rwandan church beyond any menial tasks that were planned. Do the menial tasks; they teach us about serving, and we get to serve alongside our brothers and sisters. Be sure to remember, however, that painting a room for our brothers and sisters or putting in windows isn't really what it's about. It's about meeting a deeper need in us and them.

These issues aren't exclusive to short-term mission work done overseas. I recently talked with an African-American pastor from Cincinnati who said he gets an average of ten phone calls a day at Christmastime from local pastors who want to donate clothes and toys. As much as he appreciates the goodwill, he says, "No thanks. What we really need are people willing to build relationships with many of our single moms. We need tutors for kids. We need people who can have our folks over for dinner and vice versa." I sat in sadness as the pastor went on to tell me, "After hundreds of conversations like that over the last five years, only one church has taken me up on my counteroffer."

Shane Claiborne of the Simple Way in Philadelphia thinks most American Christians do care about the poor. He says, "I believe the great tragedy of the church is not that rich Christians do not *care* about the poor, but that they do not *know* the poor."[8] He believes we resort to charitable giving as a way to ease our consciences rather than really entering into mutually enriching relationships with people who are financially poor.

To Give or Not to Give?

If we think of people as "poor," we demean them. If we ignore the fact that two billion people live on less than two dollars a day, we're selfish consumers. Is there any way out of this?!

This is precisely the dilemma Boone, from Dooling's *White Man's Grave*, was feeling as he continued to experience life as an American in the world of Sierra Leone. Boone refused to be the rich American who would have African servants working for him while he looked for his Peace Corps friend Michael. Boone turned down six kids who wanted to be his servants. His African host says, "You're a millionaire. Share the wealth. For 25 cents, someone will clean your room. For a dime, someone will walk 2 miles for you to get a bucket of water for you to bathe in. Nobody here is going to admire you for not hiring servants. You'll just be thought of us unbelievably stingy."[9]

This doesn't feel quite right, does it? It brings up the same kind of dissonance I feel when I walk by homeless people who ask me for some spare change. I've heard all the arguments about how giving a dollar to homeless people perpetuates their problems rather than solving them. Yet it feels disconcerting to walk by and ignore my fellow human beings. There is a clear ethical responsibility that comes with encountering poverty.[10]

Linhart talks about how encountering poverty challenged the high school students from Indiana who traveled to Ecuador. Eighteen-year-old Amy looked over the town from her hotel and said, "It's just amazing, the poverty. Like, it breaks my heart, but it makes me feel so spoiled, and like I'm such an evil person."[11] Another student said, "Living in America is a blessing and a curse at the same time. There's a blessing because you have all this stuff, but all the stuff is a curse, you know?"[12]

Adults report the same kind of dilemma when returning from short-term mission trips. Typical comments made by adult participants include: "We're so blessed. I realize it when I see how little they have." "I'm so encouraged by how much they do with so little." "I have it so good and I never want to take it for granted after seeing the joy in these people's faces even though they have so little." My fear is that this kind of observation makes it too easy to jump on the plane in Ecuador or Ethiopia and go home convinced that "Those people are so happy just the way they are!" Here's where it can feel like a no-win situation.

On the other hand, the people of the world in great financial need possess amazing wealth in other areas. Rather than demeaning them as tragic objects to be rescued, what does it look like to see them as our equals so that we walk with them and learn from them, each benefiting from one another's "wealth" and sacrifice?[13]

Concluding Thoughts

The realities that come with money cause me a great deal of personal dissonance. Even as I write, I'm doing so from the cozy Starbucks a few blocks from my home. I'm well aware of the many whose weekly wage is equal to the cost of the latte I'm sipping. That's problematic, but how might our sympathy for fellow brothers and sisters in Christ in majority world places lead us toward treating them in demeaning ways? Our wealth creates all kinds of power issues, and as much as we want to talk about collaborative relationships between churches from one culture to another, a national leader who feels safe to be really honest with you may well confess that they realize the need to keep the "partnering" church in the West happy so that funds keep flowing.

On the other hand, we must not ease our consciences by thinking they're happy enough without our money. Maybe I need to sip a few less lattes every week and invest those same dollars to help free a couple young girls in Bangkok from prostitution. What if we committed to spend at least as much money supporting the projects we visit on our short-term trips as we do on getting us there?

The road forward requires looking at some of these tensions. The intent is not to shame you or make you feel defeated. Instead as we look honestly at the complexity of the issues related to money, our perspective begins to widen, which allows us to more effectively serve. All this perspective widening will translate into action. Changed perspective equals changed practice. We'll look at that more in part 3, but first we need to look at one more reality in American short-term missions. This one overrides all the others.

Simplicity

"You're Either for Us or against Us!"

Through the eyes of Americans . . .	Through the eyes of nationals . . .
It was unbelievable. They treated us like rock stars. The Brazilians were like storming the stage, asking for our autographs and chasing our buses. I don't think they get to see Americans very often.	This was all a big joke one of our Brazilian friends started. We pretended they were famous by storming the stage and asking for their autographs. But we live in Sao Paulo—one of the most cosmopolitan cities in the world. We've seen plenty of Americans.

President George W. Bush will be chronicled in history books for his frequently repeated statement to the world, "You're either with us or you're for the terrorists."[1]

I've talked with more than a few non-Western friends who are perplexed by his statement, and even more, the thinking behind it. One of my Asian friends said, "We don't for a second embrace the domination by terrorists who pillage the homes of harmless families and carelessly kill thousands. We watched with horror what happened to your country on September 11. On the other hand, we can't support the dominance of the 'American dream' for the world. We've observed the complacency of the United States in Sudan, Tibet, and Rwanda, and it's hard to entirely get behind this current campaign, especially without more global input."

Filmmaker Michael Moore appears to exercise the same kind of oversimplification for which he so brutally attacks Bush in his documentary film *Fahrenheit 9/11*. Moore asked Pete Townshend, British rock star of The Who, for permission to use his anthem "Won't Get Fooled Again" as part of the soundtrack for *Fahrenheit 9/11*. Townshend refused because he felt that Moore's previous works demonstrated "bullying" and lack of good critical engagement with key issues. In response Moore accused Townshend of being a war supporter. Townshend says Moore's attitude seemed like the very terrorist credo he was criticizing in Bush: "If you're not with me, you're against me."[2]

Hang on. If you think I'm headed toward a political debate in this chapter, I'm not. For the time being I'm more interested in looking at the very American-like simplicity demonstrated by Bush and Moore alike. The simplicity conflict underlies all the others. Certainly all the areas of conflict we've considered are interrelated but this one cuts across all of them. Our conclusions about why we should go, our sense of urgency, and our use of Scripture and money all flow from our tendency to oversimplify complex issues. In particular the tendency to find common ground—wherein we tend to focus on similarities at the expense of seeing differences and where we generalize unique people and events to an entire culture—is seamlessly related to the simplicity conflict. All the other realities we've considered have important nuances worth exploring, but this one is at the core of much of the short-term mission work done by us as Americans.

Simplistic categories have been central to our American ethos. An American is either Republican or Democrat, blue-collar or white-collar, liberal or conservative, modern or postmodern, environmentalist or industrialist. Of course one of the things postmodernism has done is expose the fallacy of these clear-cut categories. There is a place for simplicity. Sometimes we can make things far too complicated and thus can never make a decision. Some areas of life and thought are clear-cut, but most of life is not. In particular most cross-cultural issues are far too complex to simply be placed in one category or another. The last several chapters were filled with countless examples of how our tendency to oversimplify affects our short-term trips—from our assumptions about the changes that occur within us and others as the result of our projects, to the ways we use Scripture to legitimize our cultural models of ministry, to our tendency to look for similarities when we encounter new people in a new place—all are nuances of the simplicity conflict. A few of the ways simplicity is directly expressed in our short-term mission work are an overuse of the K.I.S.S. principle, the rock-star complex, and the typical take-aways reported by short-term participants.

The K.I.S.S. Principle

American Christians have often embraced the K.I.S.S. (Keep It Simple, Stupid) principle for lots of different purposes. K.I.S.S. is a familiar mantra in short-term missions too, whether it's the importance of simplicity in planning your itinerary, your testimony, or your plans for follow-up. "Keep it simple," we're told.

Clearly there *is* a place for the K.I.S.S. principle. I spend a great deal of my time in university settings, and we often make things unnecessarily complicated in the academy. Overcomplexity can paralyze us and keep us from getting anywhere. But many times K.I.S.S. becomes a hindrance to cultural intelligence. If we live only by the K.I.S.S. principle and never ask the deeper questions, we're at risk of missing some core issues, particularly in cross-cultural work. We'll keep it simple, but remain stupid.

When we explored our tendency to seek common ground, we looked at how easily we inaccurately interpret familiar behaviors. Short-termers assume smiling, nodding, and silence mean the same things for all people. Likewise the way we too quickly generalize the behavior of one person to everyone in a culture is another demonstration of the K.I.S.S. principle negatively at work.

I first became aware of the prevalence of the K.I.S.S. principle in short-term work when I began asking short-term participants what they observed about the new context being visited. When I asked, "What's the number-one thing that stands out in your mind from what you experienced in this new cultural context?" I most often heard these kinds of responses, from both adults and youth:

- "People were driving on the wrong side of the road. That was the first thing I noticed, as well as the foreign language of course, and having to figure out their money."
- "I always notice the children most. I never get used to seeing these young kids have to beg for food. It's so unfair that kids have to grow up there."
- "It's not as modern as things here. They don't have jetways at the airports and they aren't very organized. That's what I notice."
- "The buildings and cars are different. . . . They don't have standards for that kind of stuff like we do."
- "The poverty is what I notice the most. It's hard to believe people live in conditions like that. And they have chain-link fences everywhere."
- "I just notice how happy everyone is. They have so little but they're so happy."

Hopefully you're seeing the familiarity of many of these themes from things we've been looking at throughout the last several chapters. More than anything else, I hope the findings reported in this book help us move away from using the K.I.S.S. principle as our guiding protocol for short-term work. Simplistic categories that lump everything into one category or the other, or look at only the obvious surface-level issues, are not helpful in bringing about effective work cross-culturally. Requiring a PhD in intercultural studies for every short-term mission participant is not what I'm after. However, we have to open our eyes to some of the things happening below the surface. We'll go after some suggestions on how to get there in the next section of the book—cultural intelligence (CQ). Before we get there, though, let's look at a couple of the other ways we tend to oversimplify our thinking in short-term missions.

Rock-Star Complex

Another way simplicity frequently gets played out is the presence of a rock-star complex when we go cross-culturally for a few days. The rock-star complex is another way to describe ethnocentrism—the tendency to define what's normal and best based upon our cultural perspective. It's the assumption that the world revolves around us. Here are a couple ways I've seen ethnocentrism or the rock-star complex get played out on short-term trips.

A few years ago, I attended a church service in the Chicago area where a youth group was reporting on their recent two-week trip to Sao Paulo, Brazil. The youth group had done a number of musical and dramatic presentations in public schools, churches, and shopping centers throughout Sao Paulo. The team of students and adults described the typical things heard from a group like this, including the ways their hearts were stretched by the generosity and contentment of the people, the challenge to consider missions as a vocation, and the need for us to pray for the struggling, small Brazilian churches.

Another theme present throughout most of the testimonials was the students describing how strange it was to be treated like rock stars whenever they completed one of their performances. One student said, "It was unbelievable. They treated us like rock stars. The Brazilians were like storming the stage, asking for our autographs and chasing our buses as we drove away. I don't think they get to see Americans very often."

A few weeks after attending this service, I met with a couple Brazilian teenagers who were in Chicago for a yearlong exchange student program. These Brazilians were attending the Chicago-area church that had just sent the group to Sao Paulo and they saw the American group perform when they came down to Brazil. Given my interest in comparing North American perceptions of short-term experiences with those who receive them, I asked them what they observed about the American group while they were there. The Brazilian teenagers spoke warmly of the friendships they developed, particularly since they themselves were now on the other side of cross-cultural travel. They talked about the joy they experienced as they heard the testimonies and music from these American students.

After the Brazilian students spent a lot of time affirming the American group, I jumped in and said, "Tell me about their perception of being treated like rock stars." My new Brazilian friends immediately started laughing and blushing. After insisting they tell me what was so funny, they said, "Don't tell them because we would feel really bad. But this was all a big joke one of our Brazilian friends started. He decided we'd make them think they were famous and everything by storming the stage, asking for their autographs, getting their pictures and that kind of stuff. I mean we live in Sao Paulo—one of the most cosmopolitan cities in the world. We've seen plenty of Americans. Don't get me wrong. We enjoyed their music and drama and stuff, but they weren't exactly 'rock stars' in our eyes."

For those wanting to write off the rock-star complex as youthfulness, I haven't seen a significant difference among adults who go overseas on short-term trips. This is the same tendency that drove the American pastors to confidently claim, "They're so hungry for our training" and "We have a biblical model that applies to everyone."

Some of the more jaded people with whom I've talked about this rock-star syndrome have said, "Come on. This isn't some unique thing going on in cross-cultural work. This is pride. It's arrogance. That's what these kids are doing when they think everyone wants their autographs. That's what these pastors are doing when they assume everyone wants their training."

I'm not so sure! Okay, certainly all of us as human beings struggle desperately with wanting to prove ourselves, and we long to be significant. So in that regard, clearly some threads of arrogance weave through these kinds of behaviors. But I think this is more than pride.

One of the things that confounded me most in my study of North American pastors' cross-cultural training experiences was the difference between what they said before they went on their trips and how they behaved when they got there. In my conversations with them prior to their trips, they espoused and demonstrated a strong spirit of humility. They weren't the self-absorbed people they might appear to be when looking at their cold, cocky comments written on a page, without a face. Likewise most of the high school students I talk to about their mission trips are conscious of wanting to be learners. So why do they still end up being so ethnocentric and colonialist in their cross-cultural work? Why do they come off with a rock-star complex? I think it comes back to the issue of simplicity. As Americans in particular, and now I'm the one generalizing, we as a whole are not inclined to reflective thinking beyond surface-level observations. The K.I.S.S. principle drives much of how we approach cross-cultural work, so the rock-star syndrome is an inevitable result. By failing to look at the deeper issues, we come to false conclusions. Hopefully this is helping you get closer to seeing why a changed perspective is essential to short-term missions.

Take-Aways

One more way our simplicity is blatantly evident in our short-term work is that we repeat, with amazing regularity, the same take-aways from these trips. It's as if we've been scripted with the "right answers" for what we learned from the trip. We parrot one another with statements like these:

"We have it so good here."
"We're so caught up in materialism."
"We need to pray more."
"I felt so close to God there. He's doing amazing things there."

With little variation, these are the things reported in follow-up letters and given in testimonials. When I asked Rhonda, a thirty-year-old woman, how her experience in East Africa changed her, she said, "We have so much and they have so little. That's a plus for us because we're so blessed. I mean, we all have running water, electricity, telephones, computers, and cars that go down the street with no problem. And the power doesn't go out. . . . But our material possessions can be a hindrance because they keep us from really focusing on God."

Bill, a fifty-two-year-old pastor from Southern California, said, "I was really encouraged to see how they deal with so little and how strong their faith is. That makes my needs in life and ministry seem so small comparatively, or at least different."

Shannon, a twenty-seven-year-old woman, said, "I never want to forget some of the things I've seen this last week. These people do so much with so little. I have it so good."

Ken, a thirty-year-old man, said, "The biggest thing I learned was the power of prayer."

These adults' reflections are largely reminiscent of what teenagers have to say about their experiences. Remember eighteen-year-old Amy's comment: "It's just amazing the poverty. Like, it breaks my heart, but it makes me feel so spoiled, and like I'm such an evil person."[3] More than two-thirds of the high school students I've surveyed about their mission trips have said something like fifteen-year-old Ryan: "I just felt so close to God when I was there. I wish I could keep that feeling alive at home, but I know I won't."[4]

In many ways these are rich, potentially life-changing conclusions. Exposure to what God is doing among other believers around the world, raising consciousness about our wealth and the trappings thereof, and suspending "life as normal" for a few days as a way to deepen intimacy with God—who can argue with that?

However, one of the more troubling comments I heard from a group of majority world pastors who were giving me their frank perspective on American short-term trips was this: "You talk about us to your churches back home in such demeaning ways."

I pushed back. "Really?! You guys come off as heroes in the reports I hear. You would think your churches were near perfect from what most short-termers say about you."

They weren't so sure. Our exaggerations about how nationals are so dependent upon these short-term teams, the long-term impact suggested by the work, the jokes about the weird foods given and the destitute conditions, and the exaggerated reports about what was accomplished often lead our brothers and sisters to feel demeaned.

I'm troubled by the way our simplicity plays out in redundant statements about what's happened in our lives as a result of our short-term sojourns. I expected more, particularly out of the adults, and especially the pastors. While we describe the dissonance we feel as we see our wealth juxtaposed against poverty, it seems to have little influence upon the number of souvenirs we purchase or the choices we make when we get home. Participants rarely describe a significant change in how they think about God and their faith as a result of trips like these. In fact, rather than being challenged to see Christianity differently, participants talk most about the reminder that Christ and his bride are the same everywhere.

All too often, the short-term experience "eludes any significant reflection on the deeper assumptions and attitudes that structure one's view of God, of themselves, and of host strangers."[5] Linhart reports that the Indiana group he studied demonstrated an "absence of theological reflection about their ministry programs they were conducting, no attempts to understand the incongruity between poverty and joy, and no awareness of new experiences that contradicted previous observations or interpretations."[6]

Clearly there *are* participants who experience deep transformation and come home with very different descriptions of what's occurred within them. But why aren't there more? Why are our take-aways always the same, surface-level things? What can we do to make long-term transformation more common among the million or more Americans who do short-term missions overseas every year?

Concluding Thoughts

Our assumptions about what happens as a result of short-term missions are oversimplified. As a result our expectations and motivations are inaccurate. Our desire to "Just do it" comes from a short-term perspective rather than a long-term vision. Our tendency to look for similarities often keeps us from seeing differences, and as a result we miss out on the more colorful picture that exists among the people of the world. Our reduction of the Bible to manageable concepts and cultural principles sucks the life out of the story of God. Our simplistic approaches to help poor people end up exposing our own poverty. Simplicity is endemic to short-term missions. It's part of what it means to be an American. It's part of what it means to be an American evangelical. But it doesn't have to be.

There's an endearing simplicity to Jesus's focus as he goes about his ministry. Yet a quick perusal of his use of parables and his upside-down approach to challenging the established religious system ought to warn any of us against labeling Jesus as the epitome of simplicity. Our response should not be to see how complicated we can make short-term missions, much less life. Instead we must acknowledge that we aren't going to be content to simply look at what we can see with a quick glance. We've been on a journey to open our eyes wider in order to see what we may have missed before. Are you beginning to see it? Is your vision broadening?

Part 3

Sharpening Our Focus and Service with Cultural Intelligence (CQ)

What do we make of all this? Do we throw up our arms in despair, cut up our passports, and throw out every letter soliciting funds for short-term missions? Believe me, there have been many times when I have been more than ready to go there. I have countless pages in my journals over the last several years where I wrote entries like this one:

> Is all the money and effort invested in short-term work paying off? As short-termers, we're often ill-equipped to solve the real needs that exist in the places we visit. Locals are enduring our water bottles and weak stomachs, and we're spending millions of dollars to do it. Is there a way to truly make short-term missions a win-win?[1]

At the end of the day, I'm not convinced we're without hope in seeing short-term missions as an effective tool for serving

God's church globally. If criticisms alone are enough reason to abandon the entire movement, then let's be consistent. Let's also abandon all career missions and support of nationals, because we're not short on criticisms and bad behavior in those expressions of global missions either. Clearly we can't go there, or we fail to fulfill the central call of God upon his people—to extend his reign among all the nations. I'm committed to seeing us redeem short-term missions. How might we engage in short-term missions with eyes wide open and use it as a way to widen our perspective? It's time to move to the final section of this journey together—looking at what it means to do short-term missions with cultural intelligence (CQ). CQ is a tool to help us translate our widened perspective into better missional practice.

Don't be frightened by the technical sound of something like CQ. CQ is just a way of measuring our ability to interact effectively when we cross cultures. The theory was developed recently using some of the same ideas used to develop IQ, EQ, and the theory of multiple intelligences. We often are told there's little we can do to change our IQ. Fortunately CQ isn't like that. It's something that *can* be learned and developed over time, and the materials in this section are a way to begin your journey of becoming more culturally intelligent. By the way, you're already on your way. One of the biggest steps toward enhancing your CQ is simply to open your eyes to the realities of the world and to the challenges of cross-cultural interactions—that's what we've spent the last several chapters exploring.

Don't try to attain some perfect CQ score (which doesn't really exist) by the time you go on your next trip. Our CQ is continually moving and growing. So our desire is simply to use the last section of this book to embark on a lifelong journey of growing in CQ as a way to more effectively love God and others in the twenty-first-century world. CQ will help us sharpen our focus and service in short-term missions, and it can enhance our missional living wherever we are, all the time.

CQ is a matrix that consists of four different emphases, all of which are linked together. As demonstrated in figure 1, the four interconnected elements of CQ are: (1) knowledge CQ, (2) interpretive CQ, (3) perseverance CQ, and (4) behavioral CQ. Most materials designed for short-term work emphasize the kinds of things covered by two of the CQ components—knowledge CQ (cross-cultural understanding) and behavioral CQ (cross-cultural behavior). But all four components are needed for effective short-term missions. The interdependence of these four factors is important, because having one without the others may actually be worse than having none of them.[2]

The next four chapters will describe the four elements of the CQ matrix. I define each of the CQ factors, suggest some ways to nurture growth in each of them, and demonstrate what they look like in real life by going on a journey to Shanghai, China, with a group of college students.[3] Let me take a minute and briefly define the four elements before moving into the expanded descriptions of each of them in the chapters that follow.

Knowledge CQ: Understanding Cross-Cultural Differences

Knowledge CQ, or cognitive CQ as it's called in the original research, measures our level of knowledge and *understanding* about cross-cultural differences.

Interpretive CQ: Interpreting Cues

Interpretive CQ, or meta-cognitive CQ as it's called in the original research, measures our ability to accurately *interpret* cues we receive as we engage cross-culturally.

Perseverance CQ: Persevering through Cross-Cultural Conflict

Perseverance CQ, or motivational CQ as it's called in the original research, measures our degree of interest in *persevering* through cross-cultural conflict.

Behavioral CQ: Acting Appropriately

Behavioral CQ, which is what it's also called in the original research, measures our ability to actually *act* appropriately when interacting cross-culturally.

Figure 1

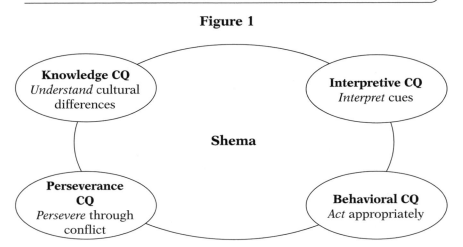

Seek to Understand

Knowledge CQ

Eight Christian college students left their dorm rooms in Indiana to spend their January term in Shanghai, China. The team are all TESL (Teaching English as a Second Language) students who thought this experience would give them hands-on experience at TESL and serve as a mission trip. They raised support from family and friends, billing it as a chance to share the gospel with Chinese peers who wanted to learn English. The team was led by Jake, a senior marketing major with a minor in TESL. Jake grew up as a missionary kid in Mexico. He's spent more time living outside the United States than in it.

The group's Chinese host was Tan Jun. After picking the American students up at the airport, Jun took them to a crowded Shanghai restaurant. Fortunately for the team, Jun spoke flawless English. After they were seated at the restaurant, Jun smiled and said, "Perhaps you're tired after your long journey."

Jake, the team leader, said, "Yeah, we're pretty wasted, but it will be good to eat something other than plane food!"

Jun continued to smile and said, "Well, I hope you're okay with the food here. I can't say it's the very best at this restaurant, but hopefully, it should be okay."

Jake, again on behalf of the group, blurted out, "Hey. We'll make the best of it. It's all part of the adventure!" Jun's smile seemed to fade slightly.

Jenny, one of the other team members, was trying to silently unpack what she thought Jun was trying to communicate. She had just taken a course in intercultural communication, so she felt like something might be going on here that deserved attention. She began to wonder, *Is criticizing the food just a typical Chinese custom—something everyone does that really has nothing to do with the food itself?* Or maybe he was trying to make a joke. She remembered that humor was one of the hardest things to translate cross-culturally. But Jun did have a big smile as he said it, so maybe he was trying to be funny. On the other hand, in the brief synopsis she had read about Chinese culture, she knew they made a practice of self-effacing. So perhaps that's what this was. Or was it the indirect approach often used by Chinese people when they interact? Or maybe this was Jun's backhanded way of expressing concern about whether the next three weeks of working together was a good idea.[1]

Just then Jenny realized Jun was talking to her. "What are you studying?" he asked her.

She replied, "Oh—I'm majoring in communications and I might minor in TESL." Then she said, "I heard you just graduated with an English major, Jun. What are you going to do next?"

"Oh. I already have a job at the university," he said.

"Congratulations. Have you found a place to live?" she asked.

"Actually, the university is right by my house," Jun replied.

"You mean your parents' house?" asked Jenny.

"Yes. Exactly. Our house," replied Jun.

"So are you going to save up some money for awhile before you move out?" chimed in Jake.

Jun replied, "No. We're quite happy with our place."

Jake said, "Well, I guess that's not all bad until you're married anyway."

Jun said, "I am married."

Sarah, the only student on the team majoring in intercultural studies, said, "Oh yeah. All Asians do that." A couple of the other students rolled their eyes, both because they had been listening to Sarah's expertise on Asian culture every few minutes for the last thirty hours, and because they couldn't imagine the thought of living with their parents after being married.

Jenny's mind began to wander again. *Why do so many generations here live together? That can't be healthy for marriage, can it? Or maybe we're the ones who aren't healthy by thinking we have to get out on our own.*

"Jenny!" Jake interrupted her thoughts. "The rice, please. Can you please pass the rice?"

A myriad of things occurred in these first few minutes the American students spent with their Chinese host. At the surface level, Jenny's concerns are connected to her limited understanding of Chinese customs. As compared to Jake, who seems not even to observe that some miscommunication might be occurring, Jenny is aware something isn't quite right, but she lacks the cultural intelligence to know what it is and how best to respond. How do we explain Sarah? We haven't heard much from her, but it appears the rest of the team has. Is she demonstrating the greatest measure of knowledge CQ because she's devoted almost all her study to intercultural issues? We'll come back to these students in Shanghai in a bit. But let's stop and look at this first component of cultural intelligence—knowledge CQ.

In recent years, a great deal of attention has been given to the importance of predeparture training for people who are going to participate in short-term work. Leaders spend time preparing groups for what they should expect when they travel to the destination. While some groups spend only a few minutes looking at a description of where they're headed, others invest time researching the history of the place, their people's views on religion, their language, and more. This, in part, is what growing our knowledge CQ means.

What Is Knowledge CQ?

Knowledge CQ simply refers to our understanding about crosscultural issues and differences. While this understanding includes the kinds of things done in many short-term orientation meetings, it's also more than just learning about the history and stereotypes of a culture. The most important part of knowledge CQ is gaining general information about how cultures vary. Explicitly and implicitly, how does culture affect the way people view the world? How does that relate to the specific culture we're about to visit? How does it explain our own behavior? What's behind the common gestures used? These are the type of questions a person with knowledge CQ asks and understands. Growing in knowledge CQ requires more than simply reading the *Lonely Planet Guide* for the country we're about to visit; it involves an ongoing process of looking at cultures and beginning to understand how they vary.

In talking about how to grow in our understanding of culture, it's important to consider a definition of culture. Anthropologists and sociologists have argued for years about how to define culture, but most agree that culture is the collective fundamental beliefs people hold about how things should be and how one should behave. It's a way of looking at the values, attitudes, and beliefs shared by a common group of people. While such things as food, art, and literature give us visible expressions of culture, one of the greatest challenges that comes with gaining understanding about culture is that cultural knowledge is largely invisible. So when we talk about serving with eyes wide open, the vision we're trying to enhance is not primarily our physical eyesight but the ability to open our eyes to see what isn't immediately visible to the physical eye. It's looking beyond the driving habits, diet, and architecture to see what lies beneath those things. That's what knowledge CQ allows us to do.

Think of culture as the software that runs our minds. It's the mental programming that shapes our habits, beliefs, decision making, and the way we see the world.[2] This programming is passed along from generation to generation. Cultural programming applies to national and ethnic groups, to organizations (such as the culture of a particular company or church), and even to subcultural groups such as adolescents, homosexuals, or evangelicals. While knowledge CQ can enhance interactions in any of these cultural groups, our interest is in national culture—seeking to understand the socioethnic cultures of people living in the communities we're visiting on our short-term trips.

An easy way to see how culture programs our minds is to look at the different views people from different cultures have of dogs. My thoroughly American daughter Emily loves dogs more than anyone I know. She loves to pet them, feed them, walk them, and cuddle with them. If she had her way, our home would be filled with dogs. Unfortunately for her, I'm not yet convinced our family is ready to have a dog. However, Emily, like many Westerners, sees dogs not as mere animals but as members of the family. Even those of us who aren't dog lovers think of dogs as belonging in people's homes and yards. As Americans, dogs eat with us, watch TV with us, and go on vacation with us. It's becoming more and more common in suburbs around the country to find boutiques devoted exclusively to dogs. In contrast, many people living in Islamic cultures view dogs as animals to be avoided at all costs. They see dogs like the typical American sees rats or pigs. In their minds dogs are dirty animals that are primarily a nuisance. In still other parts of the world, dogs are considered an important and preferred part of one's diet—literally—and I'm not talking about "hot dogs."

Which is the "right" view of dogs? These are the kinds of places where we can be tempted to misuse the Bible. American dog lovers might find a verse that proves their view of dogs. Certainly there are values (and verses!) that direct how we should treat all animals, including dogs. But we're hard-pressed to make a biblical case for or against any of these cultural differences in how people view dogs. That might seem so wrong to you, because our view of dogs is so ingrained in us through the mental programming of our culture.

Knowledge CQ helps us move beyond seeing the stray dogs roaming throughout Indonesia as simply neglected pets and calls us to look at how Indonesians' interaction with dogs teaches us something about Indonesian culture and cultures in general. Applying knowledge CQ becomes more challenging when we're looking at issues such as how culture views polygamy or literacy or the Bible, but it's even more important with these weightier issues.

Knowledge CQ is essential because it's at the core of being able to serve with eyes wide open. Many of the pitfalls of short-term missions that we've been exploring could be avoided, or at least lessened, with growth in knowledge CQ. As we already mentioned, the point is not to master our knowledge CQ before we take off on our next trip. Knowledge CQ continues to stretch and grow throughout our lifetime. Growing in our knowledge CQ gives us a healthy starting point for more effectively engaging in short-term mission. As we'll point out throughout each of the CQ factors, knowledge CQ by itself is not enough. In some cases, growing our knowledge CQ without growing the other CQ elements might be worse than never growing our knowledge CQ in the first place. I'll explain that more in a minute. Given that the ideal is that we *will* grow in our knowledge CQ, along with the other components, let's look at some important considerations for nurturing knowledge CQ in others and ourselves.

Nurturing Knowledge CQ

How do we nurture our understanding about cultural differences? If we're going to Mexico, reading about some of the basic habits of Mexican people isn't a bad starting point. In order to truly nurture our knowledge CQ however, we need to go beyond that. We need to look at a broader perspective of cultural understanding by exploring some key categories of cross-cultural difference. Keep in mind that knowledge CQ is not primarily about mastering the dos and don'ts of a particular culture. Instead it's understanding some of the rudimentary dynamics and differences that exist between cultures. Beware. We don't want to be overly influenced by the simplicity issue and simply reduce all cultural variances into a few categories. However, categories can be the very tool to help us move beyond oversimplification. As we think about nurturing our knowledge CQ, we'll look at five different dimensions used to help understand and measure cultural difference—time, context, individualism, power distance, and uncertainty avoidance. Many more than these exist, but these are the most helpful ones for nurturing knowledge CQ, particularly for short-term mission trips.

Event Time vs. Clock Time

Most of us are pretty familiar with the way people from different cultures view time. We can easily think of cultures where people are routinely punctual and those where people are chronically "late." While not wanting to oversimplify or stereotype people too quickly, this kind of understanding is precisely what we're after in developing knowledge CQ. Tapping into your understanding about cultures and time takes you farther down the road to nurturing your knowledge CQ.

In his book *A Geography of Time*, Robert Levine[3] explores the role of industrialization in how a culture views time. According to Levine, industrialization promotes an ethos of producing and consuming. As a result, people in those cultures live by "clock time." Punctuality and efficiency rule the day. A great deal of what we considered as part of the "urgency" issue in part 2 is an expression of our clock-time orientation. The clock is what determines when things start and end. Respect, excellence, and conscientiousness are communicated by our punctuality.

In contrast, less-industrialized cultures are far more interested in emphasizing the priority and obligation of social relationships. Levine refers to these cultures as "event-time" cultures. Events begin and end when all the participants feel the time is right rather than artificially imposing clock time. Spontaneity is a core value among these people. A South American talked about the birthday party he threw for his son while they were living in the United States. They invited friends from the United States and some friends from Latin America. The invitation said the party would be from 2:00 to 4:00 p.m. on Saturday. The friends from the United States showed up at 2:00 and left around 4:00. In contrast, several of the Latins came thirty to ninety minutes late and stayed well past 4:00 p.m. Some of them remained until 2:00 the next morning. One Argentinean friend asked the father why the invitation listed an ending time. He was offended by the implication that there was a time limit on how long they could be together.[4]

What's the time orientation of people in the culture you're visiting on your short-term trip? Understanding alone can't prepare you for all the challenges that might come with opposing views of time, but it's a good start. If you're going with a team of people, spend some time anticipating how your approach to time might frustrate the locals who host you. How might their time orientation frustrate you?

High Context vs. Low Context

One of the most common categories used to describe cultures is high-context versus low-context cultures. Again, though artificial, understanding these categories can enhance our knowledge CQ. High context refers to places where people have a lot of history together. Things operate in high-context cultures as if everyone there is an insider and knows how to behave. Written instructions and explicit directions are minimal because most people know what to do and how to think.

Our families are probably the most tangible examples we have of high-context environments. After years of being together, we know what the unspoken rules are of what we eat, how we celebrate holidays, and how we communicate with each other. Many of our church cultures are the same. We know when to sit, stand, and participate. Some national cultures are high-context too. In places such as Latin America, Korea, and the Middle East, information is much more likely to be assumed and embedded within people rather than explicitly stated. There aren't a lot of signs or detailed information about how to act. High-context cultures are difficult places to visit as an outsider.

Places such as Western Europe and the United States are categorized as low-context cultures. Many of our connections with particular people and places are of a shorter duration, therefore less is assumed. Instructions about where to park, how to flush the toilet, and where to order your food are often displayed. Low-context cultures can be easier to enter than high-context cultures, because even if you're an outsider, much of the information needed to participate is explicit. Extra attention is given to providing information about how to act.[5]

Spend some time thinking about how your short-term trip will be affected by whether you're headed to a high-context or low-context environment. As Americans we're often frustrated by life in a high-context environment. Signs at the airport might seem unclear, and locals might spend little time giving us instructions about how to order in a restaurant. But as we begin to see the realities of high and low contexts, we begin to grow our knowledge CQ.

Individualism

The next three areas come from the work of Geert Hofstede, a researcher who studied the cultural differences of a hundred thousand IBM employees spread out over fifty countries. The first of these areas is individualism.[6]

One day some friends in Singapore were explaining to me how Singaporean students are put in career tracks as early as fourth or fifth grade. Teachers assess students' areas of strength, such as writing or math, and begin to groom them for vocations that match those strengths. As a result, by the time Singaporean students get ready to graduate from high school, it's pretty clear what path they're going to take—whether medicine, teaching, or technology. However, the universities and technical institutes have a limited number of openings for each area, so after the quotas are reached for premed students or education students, for example, young people are directed into other career paths.

As I listened to this, I aborted any sense of cultural intelligence and said, "That's so unfair! Why can't the Singaporean system empower people to pursue their dreams instead of prescribing everyone's future?"

They listened to me continue my rant then calmly responded, "You're assuming we place as much importance on personal dreams and goals as Americans do. For us, the individual is not what's most important. Our collective society is what we value. If we have an overabundance of physicians and a shortage of teachers, we won't be sustained as a society. If there aren't enough people in the technical workforce, we'll be overrun by other, much larger countries."

While I'm not ready to entirely abandon allowing people to pursue some measure of personal calling, I saw in front of my eyes what it looks like to understand my individualist orientation versus their collectivist orientation.

The United States scored ninety-one out of a hundred points on Hofstede's scale of individualism, as compared to Singapore's score of twenty. Cultures that score high on the individualism scale are places where people are most concerned about the life of the individual. Decisions are based upon what the individual deems is best for his or her life. Nowhere is this more apparent than in our own culture. Nowadays, the American dream seems less characterized by having a four-bedroom house with a white picket fence, a minivan, and 2.5 kids than by getting to the place where you can say, "I'll think what I want, do what I want, go where I want, and be responsible to no one but myself."

In contrast, countries that score low on the individualism scale are called "collectivist" cultures. In these places, people view themselves less autonomously and more as members of groups. They're concerned about the effects of actions upon the group as a whole, and decisions are made by consensus rather than individualistically. This isn't to say people living in collectivist cultures are purely unselfish. Rather they're programmed to think about the goals and needs of the groups of which they're a part rather than to consider their own individual needs first.

Neither end of the continuum is a complete picture of how God calls us to live. Something about our attention on the individual coincides with the personal responsibility God gives us. Jesus seems very interested in individuals as well as entire families and nations. He calls people to personally follow him. At the same time, our obsession with our needs and wants and our quest for personal spiritual growth is not a complete reflection of how we're to live. Scripture is full of examples where God speaks to communities rather than to individuals. For example, almost every reference to "spiritual maturity" in the New Testament is to a plural audience. I'm not called to resist sin or pursue God by myself, and the goal of my spiritual maturity isn't just for me. I'm called to mature *with* my brothers and sisters in the faith, *for* the sake of my brothers and sisters in the faith—both my local church community and the community of God's people all over the world—past, present, and future.

As we begin to open our eyes to the varying ways cultures view the individual, we begin to see an important area that affects our knowledge CQ. The college students listening to Jun talk about living with his parents considered first and foremost what Jun would want for himself rather than considering what might be best for his entire family. Furthermore Jun didn't seem to pick up that the students found his living situation unusual. A greater measure of understanding about the varying beliefs cultures have about individuals and groups such as families could increase the cultural intelligence of the American students and Jun.

Power Distance

Power distance refers to how "far apart" leaders and followers feel from each other. Countries that score high in power distance—such as Mexico, India, and Ghana—offer a great deal of formal respect to leaders. Titles and status are revered, leaders and followers are unlikely to socialize together, and subordinates are not expected to question their superiors.

Linda and I have had African friends in our home who are amazed at the amount of voice we give our girls in everyday decisions. It's second nature for us to give them a choice of cereal in the morning, let them pick out the clothes they're going to wear, offer them options of things we could do together on the weekend, and encourage them to ask the "why" question. We as Americans score much lower on the power-distance scale than most African cultures do.

International students from high power-distance cultures who come to study in the United States often demonstrate their discomfort with the different attitudes toward authority figures from what they see at home. A student from Iran said, "The first time my professor told me, 'I don't know the answer—I will have to look it up,' I was shocked. I asked myself, 'Why is he teaching me?' In my country a professor would give a wrong answer rather than admit ignorance."[7]

A student from Indonesia, a culture that scores even higher than Iran in power distance, made this comment: "I was surprised and confused when on leaving Whittier Hall the provost, in person, held the door for me in order to let me pass before he would enter the door. I was so confused that I could not find the words to express my gratefulness, and I almost fell on my knees as I would certainly do back home. A man who is by far my superior is holding the door for me, a mere student and a nobody."[8]

The United States is by no means the lowest on the scale of power distance. Our score is forty, and trailing behind us are Canada, Germany, and Finland. Austria and Israel, with respective scores of eleven and thirteen, are among the countries lowest in power distance. In these contexts, followers feel at ease socializing with their leaders and addressing them as peers. Students feel free to question their pastors, teachers, and parents, and they expect to have input in the decision-making process.

I have little patience for top-down, directive styles of leadership. I'm much more comfortable with an egalitarian approach that leads through team and creates vision with the input of many voices. However, I must be careful not to allow my cultural background in power distance to be biblicized. Obviously the Bible has much to say about the importance of serving and of sharing leadership. However, we have to avoid proof-texting team-based approaches to leadership that are really more culturally based than biblically based. The same applies to those more inclined toward high power distance. Are the hierarchical forms of leadership in the Bible an outgrowth of the respective cultures where they took place or directives intended by God?

Considering the relationship between so-called high-status people and low-status people, and between leaders and followers, is an important area where we must continue to grow in understanding. The short-term participants who engage in cultural intelligence will avoid writing off a leadership style they observe cross-culturally, but instead will seek to understand it.

Uncertainty Avoidance

Finally, the uncertainty-avoidance dimension measures the extent to which a culture is at ease with the unknown. Cultures that score high on uncertainty avoidance are places where people have been programmed to have little tolerance for the unknown. They focus on ways to reduce uncertainty and ambiguity, and they create structures to help ensure some measure of predictability. For example, cultures such as Greece, Japan, and France want clear instructions and predictable timetables for completing assignments in order to reduce any ambiguity.

On the other hand, cultures low in uncertainty avoidance, such as Britain, Jamaica, and Sweden, are not as threatened by unknown situations and what lies ahead. Open-ended instructions, varying ways of doing things, and loose deadlines are more typical in countries with low scores in uncertainty avoidance.

Obviously this dimension has a high level of correlation with the way a culture approaches time. Clock-time cultures tend to be higher on the uncertainty-avoidance scale than event-time cultures, but not necessarily. This particular dimension also is a way to understand the differences that exist between two cultures that might otherwise seem to be much the same. For example, Germany and Great Britain have a great deal in common. Both are in Western Europe, both speak a Germanic language, both had relatively similar populations before the German reunification, and the British royal family is of German descent. Yet the person with knowledge CQ who understands the uncertainty-avoidance dimension will quickly notice considerable differences between life in Frankfurt and life in London. Punctuality, structure, and order are modus operandi in German culture, whereas Brits are much more easygoing and less concerned about precision. This can be explained in part due to the different views the cultures have toward the unknown.

Take a look at how a few of these countries scored in these five areas.

Key Dimensions of Cross-Cultural Differences[9]

Country or Region	High vs. Low Context	Time Orientation	Individualism	Power Distance	Uncertainty Avoidance
Australia	Low	Clock	90	36	51
Brazil	High	Event	38	69	76
East Africa Region	High	Event	27	64	52
France	Mid	Clock	72	68	86
Great Britain	Mid	Clock	89	35	35
India	High	Event	48	77	40
Israel	Low	Event	54	13	81
Mexico	High	Event	30	81	82
Thailand	High	Clock	20	64	64
USA	Low	Clock	91	40	46

Obviously these are huge generalizations. For example, while Australians are listed as having a clock-time orientation, someone observing the South Sea Islanders in Australia would find this laughable. The South Sea Islanders are very much oriented by event time. Similar exceptions exist in each of the countries or regions listed. Regardless, this chart begins to provide some sense of the differences we must understand to strengthen our knowledge CQ.

Exploring the differences between how people view time, status, and uncertainty are the types of issues central to developing knowledge CQ. One of the most effective ways to think through and understand the implications of these dynamics is to use case studies from different cultures that demonstrate how these differences play out. Books like Kohl's *Developing Cultural Awareness* and Storti's *Cross-Cultural Dialogues* are some of the best resources available for such exercises.

In addition, interactive learning, conversations, and readings related to cultural differences are helpful ways to gain understanding about cross-cultural differences. These coupled with our cross-cultural experiences provide a powerful way of nurturing knowledge CQ. We'll look more specifically at the role of travel itself in nurturing both knowledge and interpretive CQ in the next chapter. For now, suffice it to say that international experiences coupled with good information about cross-cultural differences is the most effective means of nurturing knowledge CQ.[10]

We'll have a better perspective on our short-term mission trips when we think about the values we've explored in this chapter. We need to understand both the general dimensions of cross-cultural differences and the ways those dimensions play out in the specific cultures we're going to visit. In addition, the issues we explored in part 2—motivation, urgency, common ground, the Bible, money, and simplicity—are the areas where we need to grow in our understanding of how our cultural programming as Americans affects the way we do short-term missions.

The danger of approaching knowledge CQ through the kinds of categories we've described in this chapter is that we can repeat the very pitfalls we looked at earlier, wherein we oversimplify. We can too easily ignore personality differences that are as complex as cultural differences. My wife, Linda, thrives in event-time cultures. She loves to be spontaneous and cares little about watching the clock. I find event time a welcome change for a couple days of vacation and then I'm ready to get back to structure, start-and-end times, and punctuality. Knowledge CQ has to be developed from a broader perspective than just one or two individuals. This is precisely why knowledge CQ alone does not equal cultural intelligence. It's only one of four interdependent factors.

Back in Shanghai

How might knowledge CQ shed light on what happened when Jun said, "I can't say the food is the very best at this restaurant, but hopefully it should be okay"?

What about Jun's comment about living with his parents? Sarah, the intercultural studies major, was the only one not surprised when Jun said he and his wife have no intentions of moving out. Is she the one who has knowledge CQ here?

Meanwhile, Jenny, the reflective one on the team, has enough understanding of Chinese culture to make her puzzled by Jun's apparent discomfort with the conversation. But she doesn't know how to make sense of it all. Jenny sensed something wasn't quite right.

As we move through the other elements of CQ, we'll continue to use our students' short-term mission experience in Shanghai to shed light on how CQ intersects with short-term missions. For now, we have a few different expressions of knowledge CQ among Jake, Jenny, and Sarah. Jake's had more cross-cultural experience than anyone on the team by having grown up in Mexico. So his experiential knowledge base of cross-cultural issues is pretty high. Does that make him a natural at responding to Jun? It gives him a real head start in developing knowledge CQ, but without the other three areas, there's no guarantee Jake's experience will make him any more culturally intelligent than someone who's never left the United States.

Jenny has a surface-level understanding of Chinese culture, but it does little to help her. She has some crude stereotypes about the way Chinese people tend to be indirect or self-effacing. However, she lacks the cultural intelligence to see how her individualist perspective shapes her view of Jun's living situation, and she isn't sure how to interpret the apology for the food at the restaurant.

A greater degree of knowledge CQ would have informed the students that it is customary in China to show respect for guests by disparaging one's own accomplishments, even the selection of a restaurant. In turn the guest is expected to repay this respect with a compliment. When Jake simply said, "We'll make the best of it," he made a cultural blunder with Jun.[11]

Jake, Jenny, and Sarah's various forms of preparation in understanding Chinese culture can be a powerful tool for CQ, but by themselves they aren't enough. In some cases knowledge CQ by itself can be worse than no knowledge CQ at all. Watch Sarah in the next few chapters to see what that looks like!

On Second Thought

Interpretive CQ

After dinner, Jun decided the team should take a stroll down Nanjing Road, one of the busiest shopping districts in China. The streets were mobbed with shoppers. The American students were exhilarated and exhausted all at the same time. The pollution seemed intense, and the noise level caused a major headache for several of the jet-lagged students. Jun bought them all some dumplings at a hawker stall and insisted they try them. Brian, covering his mouth as he yawned, said, "So Jun. Where are we staying tonight? Is it close to here?"

"Don't worry," replied Jun. "We'll go there after awhile. I'll show you where it is."

Brian muttered to Sarah who was walking next to him, "What I'm worried about is getting away from the stench and noise and laying down flat for the first time in thirty-two hours!"

Sarah said, "Remember, Brian, these are things Chinese people always do—stay up late, eat, and shop."

"Well, I'm not Chinese!" Brian said a little louder than he meant to.

Jun said to the students, "You live close to Chicago—yes?"

"Yeah, not too far," one of them replied.

"This looks pretty much like an American city, don't you think?" asked Jun.

The students just kind of chuckled in response.

The more tired the students became, the less difference their pretrip training seemed to have on their attitude and behavior. They were jet-lagged, tired, sweaty, queasy, and way out of their comfort zones. How does CQ affect responding to this kind of encounter? Let's look at how interpretive CQ connects with the understanding gained in knowledge CQ.

What Is Interpretive CQ?

Interpretive CQ is simply the degree to which we're mindful and aware when we interact cross-culturally. It's turning off the "cruise control" we typically use as we interact with people and intentionally questioning our assumptions. As we interpret the cues received through interpretive CQ, we continually adjust our knowledge CQ. These two elements of CQ are very dependent upon one another.

I learned how to drive on my brother's stick-shift car. I recall sitting at the traffic light, fully focused on the timing of the gas, clutch, and shift. I remember looking at the drivers in the cars around me who seemed to be doing anything *but* focusing on what they were doing. It looked like driving was second nature to them, as if their cars were on continuous cruise control.

Now that I've been driving for more than twenty years, I jump in my car and drive without thinking. I drive miles at a time without giving a second thought to what I'm doing. Sometimes I'll be driving down the highway, talking on my cell phone, and then I suddenly realize I don't have a clue where I am. It's not that I'm being entirely reckless; my mind just goes into "cruise control" as I drive along the open road.

When I drive in new places, and especially when I drive in different cultures where the rules are different, I'm much more alert. Driving on the left side of the road takes a much higher degree of mental awareness on my part. I have to suspend the mental "cruise control" and give all my attention to my driving.

When we're in our own culture, we move in and out of a lot of different kinds of interactions and events on "mental cruise control." We don't have to work extra hard to understand what someone means by a cliché they throw out or the embrace they offer before you walk away. When we interact cross-culturally, all that changes, or at least it should. We need to suspend "mental cruise control," step back, and pay close attention to the cues. That process of stepping back and becoming aware is interpretive CQ.

Interpretive CQ is the ability to connect our knowledge with what we're observing in the real world. It's developing the awareness to see and interpret cues from our cross-cultural encounters. It's all about making connections between what we know and what we're seeing and experiencing. It allows us to begin to question our assumptions as well as the assumptions of others. As we grow in interpretive CQ, we begin using cross-cultural interactions as a way to reframe how we think about particular people, circumstances, or even the world as a whole.

Let me explain interpretive CQ this way. Ang Soon, one of the lead researchers in CQ, lives and teaches in Singapore. I've traveled to Singapore a few times every year for several years. Shortly after I began exploring the field of cultural intelligence, I asked Soon if we could get together during my next visit. Though we had interacted some at a previous conference and through email, we hadn't spent much time together to this point.

She readily agreed and suggested we meet at Empires Café in the Raffles Hotel in Singapore. Raffles Hotel is in a part of town familiar to most visitors and just a block away from one of the major metro train stops. The menu at Empires Café is neatly divided between Western and Asian entrees. Knowing that I come from a low-context culture, Soon explained the menu to me and made sure I understood the Asian entrées in case I was interested. She pointed out a couple entrées in both the Western and Asian sections that she considered excellent.

We simultaneously viewed the menu and engaged in small talk. Soon asked how many times I had been to Singapore. I told her I've been visiting Singapore for several years, including some extended stays with my family.

"How do you find the local food?" she asked.

When I listed off *laksa* and *roti prata* as some of my favorites, she began to interact with me a bit differently.

Soon's initial perception of me was limited to my being an American ministry leader involved in graduate-level education and someone interested in applying CQ to mission work. Her knowledge CQ gave her some understanding of what that might mean for me. The longer she talked with me, however, the more she reframed her interactions to line up with her new assumptions about me and my familiarity with Singapore.

Soon told me she purposely chose Empires Café because she knew it would be easy to find, and she wasn't sure of my level of comfort with Asian food. Likewise she wasn't sure I would just want to eat American food, so she chose a place with both options. As we began talking, I sent her cues that demonstrated my ease with Singaporean culture. She spent less time explaining the educational system and cultural dynamics because she adjusted her assumptions about me based upon the cues she received from our interaction.

At one level, you could simply call Soon's behavior "empathetic listening," but it's more than that. Soon considered the possible cultural dynamics at work for both of us and then adjusted her assumptions from that understanding in light of our unfolding interaction together. She exercised the interpretive dimension of CQ that she spends so much time researching in others.[1]

Interpretive CQ would have helped the short-term participants we encountered in part 2. The students who assumed smiles meant everyone in Ecuador is happy would have stopped to ask if that's what the smiles really meant. Trainers who interpreted attentive students' behavior as hunger for the material would have asked whether that's what they really were communicating nonverbally.

Interpretive CQ follows a three-step process. First, interpretive CQ leads us to *plan* our cross-cultural interactions. Soon's interpretive CQ influenced the restaurant she chose for our meeting. She anticipated how to talk with me by drawing upon her understanding of what it meant to interact with an American. Short-term mission trips that involve teaching, preaching, or making any kind of presentation need planning in how to present the content specifically as it relates to the particular cultural context, as compared to how it would be taught at home. In addition, required planning must include how to most appropriately interact with authority figures and members of the opposite sex, how to approach conflict situations, and so on. Obviously the planning aspect of interpretive CQ is directly related to knowledge CQ. Understanding a culture's score in individualism or power distance aids us in planning our encounter.

Second, interpretive CQ begins to work itself out through a keen sense of *awareness* during cross-cultural interactions. Some people are naturally more observant than others, but all of us can grow in our ability to watch for cues—both explicit and implicit—sent by people and events we encounter cross-culturally. This is what Soon was doing as she listened to me describe my previous experiences in Singapore. Some of the cues I sent were subtle. I asked where she lives, and when she told me, I referenced a nearby landmark, which demonstrated to her my awareness of Singapore beyond what would be typical of the novice visitor. She became aware of my frame of reference by what I did and didn't say.

Checking and monitoring is the final step in interpretive CQ. This is when we compare what we planned with what's actually happening. If we change an assumption, we need to continually test that altered assumption with other encounters and experiences. When appropriate we can even talk about what we're observing with the people we encounter in another context. We need to exercise caution here, however. Just as we need to question our own assumptions underlying our behavior, so also we can't assume that another's perspective about their behavior is based upon accurate assumptions.

Those with high interpretive CQ possess an ongoing awareness of what's going on around them beyond what they can see with their physical eyes. They possess a mindfulness that makes them aware and thus able to more accurately interpret unfamiliar behaviors and events.

Nurturing Interpretive CQ

While all CQ elements relate to how we do short-term missions with cultural intelligence, this is the area I want to nurture most through this book. Opening our eyes to some of the subtle but real issues occurring in our short-term mission trip is the journey we've been on together. Serving with eyes wide open goes against the grain of our fast-paced, urgent culture by pausing to reflect on and question our assumptions. Reflection shouldn't mean that we simply sit off in isolation in a serene setting to write in our journals all day long. Instead we have to learn to engage in reflection and interpretation even when we're dead tired in the midst of Shanghai's city center.

The challenge is not *whether* people can think reflectively and intellectually but *how* to foster it in them. Obviously some people and cultures are more analytically inclined than others, but interpretive CQ can be nurtured and encouraged. There are a number of ways to nurture interpretive CQ, including general guidelines like those suggested by Thomas and Inkson in their book on cultural intelligence. They provide the following list as ways to pursue interpretive CQ:

- Be aware of your own assumptions, ideas, and emotions as you engage cross-culturally.
- Look for ways to discover the assumptions of others through their words and behavior.
- Use all your senses to read a situation rather than just hearing the words or seeing the nonverbals.
- View every situation from several different perspectives by using an open mind.
- Create new categories/paradigms for seeing things.
- Seek out fresh information to confirm or disconfirm new categories.
- Use empathy to try to identify.[2]

Stepping back to think reflectively and question our assumptions is one of the biggest needs in short-term mission work. Suggestions like the ones above are a good start, but we need more guidance and help in thinking about how to nurture this area that is so desperately lacking in much of our short-term work. More research is needed to carefully examine how to foster interpretive CQ, but here are some ways to begin the process:

Stimulate Your Imagination

Stimulating our imaginative capacity is one of the most important ways to nurture interpretive CQ. Stories, narratives, myths, tales, and rituals capture aspects of this world in ways not readily available with more traditional, bullet-point approaches to understanding cross-cultural differences. The dimensions we considered in nurturing knowledge CQ—individuality, power distance, and "event time" versus "clock time"—are essential starting places for effectively interacting cross-culturally. However, reading fiction and biographies of people from various cultures also will help us see the more subtle assumptions and paradigms underlying cultural values. Stimulate your imagination by reading novels and biographies about and by people in the places where you're going. Before going on your short-term mission trip, ask multiple people who live there about their favorite novels or movies. Use those to get into the mental programming of the culture.

Even if you make annual treks to the Czech Republic and want to focus all your cross-cultural understanding on the Czech context, spend some time reading pieces about and by people in other cultural contexts as well. Reading narrative pieces from a diversity of cultural perspectives will further enhance your ability to interpret cultural cues and recognize the differences. Few things enhance interpretive CQ as does this kind of reading.

If this kind of literature is new to you, let me recommend a few books. Khaled Hosseini's novel *The Kite Runner* is one of the best books I've read in the last five years. While you might not be taking a short-term trip to Afghanistan, the story written by this Afghan is sure to challenge your cultural assumptions in so many areas. Or try reading Jhumpa Lahiri's *The Namesake: A Novel* to gain perspective on the different assumptions Indian couples use in naming their children, even Indian-Americans, compared to most other Americans. I've made several references throughout this book to Richard Dooling's *White Man's Grave*. The language and witchcraft in Dooling's story is not for the lighthearted, but it's a compelling picture of life in West Africa. Of course there's also much to be gained by the true stories of Chinese pastors like Brother Yun in *The Heavenly Man* or Nelson Mandela in *The Long Walk to Freedom*.

Reading novels and biographies related to cross-cultural situations is only one way to stimulate your imagination. Actually, reading in and of itself is one of the most powerful ways to nurture our minds to think creatively and reflectively. In addition, we can stimulate our imagination by simply forcing ourselves to do routine things differently. Taking an alternate route to work, ordering a different kind of coffee, and changing the order of your morning routine will impact your ability to think outside the normal paradigms of your life. Who would have thought something so basic and simple could be part of what helps you serve with eyes wide open?

As you can see, nurturing interpretive CQ has implications that far surpass the journey of your short-term mission trip. It's the opportunity to begin viewing the world around you in new and significant ways.

Open or Close Your Window

Another way to nurture interpretive CQ comes by learning to adjust the way we interact with others. Successful communication depends upon accurately reading the cues of those with whom we interact. Introverted people reveal little and tend to keep the window into their lives closed as they interact with others. Others who are more extroverted reveal more of themselves and keep their windows open. Most of us tend to keep our window relatively small when we're in new and unfamiliar situations. In contrast, we tend to share more of ourselves when we're with people and in places where we feel safe and comfortable. With certain individuals and in certain settings, even the gregarious and extroverted are wise to open less of themselves. In other situations, even the painfully introverted need to learn to open up more as a way to appropriately interact. This communication skill is important anytime we interact with others, but it's especially important for cross-cultural conversations.

While personality differences exist throughout different cultures, cultures as a whole have a style of relating and communicating that they deem most appropriate. The person with a growing measure of interpretive CQ learns how to read cues from both individuals and a culture at large. In knowing how much of themselves to reveal, the point is not to try to be a chameleon, or to be whatever you think the other person wants you to be. Instead the point is to learn to interpret cues in order to adapt your communication and behavior in a way that puts the other person at ease. Envision yourself as a mirror to the people with whom you're speaking. What's the cadence of their speech? How loudly do they talk? What's their body language? By adjusting your behavior to mirror theirs, they'll automatically feel more comfortable. "This doesn't mean, of course, that you should be disingenuous. Rather, it shows that you're particularly sensitive to other people's emotional temperaments. You're just tweaking your style to ensure that the windows remain wide open."[3] Practice this in your next conversation.

Journal

One of the most valuable tools for nurturing interpretive CQ is journaling. Some people journal quite naturally, while others find it incredibly difficult. A lot of my research on short-term missions has included both my own journaling and reading the journals of other short-termers who graciously allowed me to do so. The majority of journals I read, however, did not demonstrate much interpretive CQ. Participants most often wrote about what they did each day, along with some prayer requests. That's a good start to journaling, but it's only the beginning of learning to journal as a way to nurture your ability to interpret cues in cross-cultural interactions.

Equally important in describing your observations is thinking about the meaning behind these observations and experiences. Writing allows us to understand our lives and others in ways that few other things do. It forces us to slow down and become aware of our surroundings. Journal writing enhances our ability to consider how to interpret the barrage of cues surrounding us during our short-term trips.

Commit to spending some time journaling on your next trip—do it before you leave, while you're there, and after you come home. Do more than simply record the events of each day. Describe things that make you uncomfortable. Write down questions that come to mind. What insights are you gaining? What are you seeing about yourself, others, and God? How might your faith be different if you had grown up in this culture instead of at home? Read your journal out loud to someone you trust. Journaling like this can be a vital source of cultural intelligence for you.

Cross-Cultural Immersions

At the risk of missing the obvious, few things have the ability to nurture interpretive CQ like our actual cross-cultural experiences. As we've seen countless times in this journey, experience alone doesn't ensure growth in our ability to interpret what's occurring cross-culturally. In fact, if we fail to engage in a reflective spirit whereby we question the assumptions of ourselves and others, immersing ourselves cross-culturally can actually be a deterrent to CQ. We can end up perpetuating erroneous assumptions and stereotypes in others and ourselves by failing to engage in interpretive CQ. Jake's experience as an missionary kid will either be an asset or a liability to his overall CQ, depending upon whether he exercises interpretive CQ.

When we seek to understand, and question whether we really understood, and question it again and again, we begin to progress in using our cross-cultural experiences themselves as a way to nurture interpretive CQ. Obviously, cross-cultural immersions are a vital source of knowledge CQ as well. Hands-on experiences in different cultures are extremely effective ways to learn about cross-cultural dynamics and differences, especially when combined with interpretive CQ. There's benefit both to continued exposure to the same place and to a variety of experiences in lots of different contexts. If interpretive CQ is high, multiple experiences in diverse settings yield some of the greatest growth in overall cultural intelligence.[4]

Don't just limit your thinking about these kinds of immersions to the encounters that happen when you're on a short-term mission trip. Cross-cultural encounters abound all around us. Watch the Spanish channel for a while, eat at a Thai restaurant, attend the Irish festival in a nearby town, interview a local migrant worker, or watch BBC news online. Few things aid us in developing interpretive CQ like cross-cultural encounters themselves.

One of the leading experts on the educational value of cross-cultural travel, Kenneth Cushner, writes, "Travel affords one to see the world from another perspective. But these lessons don't always jump right out at you. More often than not, they are missed because of one's inability to perceive what has gone on from the local perspective, or one's inability to step back from the situation."[5] We have to shut down the mental cruise control to benefit most from our travel abroad.

Don't miss the chance to use your short-term mission trip to see the world differently. Step back from the situation to interpret what's going on. That's what we're after with interpretive CQ. We're trying to reframe what we see and create new categories for understanding. In the short run, beginning to engage in strong interpretive CQ can result in a far more healthy and redemptive short-term mission trip. In the long run, stepping back to think more critically and carefully about what you observe can significantly transform the way you understand, interpret, and live out God's mission in the world. Surely that's worth the hard work of journaling, reading some good novels, and stepping back to question our assumptions.

Most short-term mission trips occur in groups. Teams go together from churches, schools, and other organizations. A key component to team members being able to engage in interpretive CQ on a short-term mission trip is the leader scheduling times for planning and reflection. The chance to dialogue with others about the cues being received and the interpretation thereof is a real asset to doing short-term missions in community rather than by yourself.

Back to Shanghai

No one seems to stand out as having a whole lot of interpretive CQ among the group meandering through Shanghai. Jake is assuming his extended experience in Mexico makes him a natural. Overall he's a confident guy who isn't very fazed by how he might come off to others, particularly in a vastly different world like China.

Sarah, the resident intercultural expert on the team, has just enough knowledge about cultures to make her dangerous. She seems to know all the answers but she isn't aware or mindful enough to be able to interpret what she's observing accurately. As a result, her high knowledge CQ, when not combined with high interpretive CQ, may actually hinder her effectiveness in China. This is something I've observed again and again. Predeparture training is vitally helpful in developing our knowledge CQ. When we fail to use it in tandem with interpretive CQ, however, it often results in worsened engagement cross-culturally than if we'd spent no time at all studying the cultural nuances. This is what my African friend Mark described to me in London when he said, "[Those American youth pastors] have prepared just enough for this trip to make them dangerous." The goal is to grow in our cross-cultural understanding and then combine that with a thoughtful, reflective spirit.

Jenny gives us the most hope for interpretive CQ of anyone on the Shanghai team. She lacks the ability to interpret what she's observing and seeing but she knows enough to stop herself and question what's really going on. With a heightened degree of knowledge CQ through more interaction with Chinese people, and by further study about how cultures relate, Jenny will be well on her way toward cultural intelligence.

Even Jun doesn't seem to be exemplary in interpretive CQ. He doesn't read many of the cues his guests are sending. The questions and yawns are the not-so-subtle attempts of the American students pleading to go to bed, but Jun doesn't pick up on the cues.

Join me in committing to work on interpretive CQ. As we learn to interpret, reflect, and reframe our observations, we create a link between our cross-cultural understanding and the actual behavior we're after in our mission work. Interpretive CQ helps connect our cultural knowledge with something deeper. Once you start down this road, it provides an ever-growing window into life as a whole. Suddenly you have a new way of seeing and approaching your faith, your interaction with people, your family, and your life. Open your eyes! Wider! Wider! Once you get a glimpse of God's world this way, you'll never want to go back to life *without* cultural intelligence.

Try, Try Again

Perseverance CQ

Brian is four months away from graduation. He hopes this trip will help him figure out how to use his TESL degree. It's been three days since the team landed in Shanghai, and this morning the team will finally begin what they came to do—teach English! As great as it's been hanging with the rest of the team, Brian didn't come here to eat squishy foods and visit temples. He came to teach English!

Jenny has taken a couple TESL courses along with her communications major. She thought TESL might be something she'd be interested in pursuing. In some ways she feels more prepared to participate in teaching the university students this week as a result of having spent some time the last couple days with some of Jun's students. On the other hand, she feels less prepared. Visiting places like the Jade Buddha Temple or the local primary school made her realize that while the students she'll be teaching are basically her peers, they've grown up with a different perspective on faith and education.

Jenny discussed this with Jake this morning on a run together. Jake said, "Jen, you've got to lighten up! You're being too hard on yourself and too analytical. People are people. I mean, most of Jun's students seem pretty much like us. For that matter, they're a whole lot like my Mexican friends back home too. I mean look at that, for example," he said, pointing to the cinema where *The Lion, the Witch, and the Wardrobe* had just started playing. "And look at that" he said, pointing to Starbucks, "and that," pointing across the street to KFC. "The world is more and more the same everywhere, and that's most true among our generation. Don't look at these students as Chinese. Just see them as people like you and me!"

"I hear what you're saying," Jen said. "But we also just ran by a local restaurant serving cat for lunch, and every store has an altar in front. That's nothing like the world back home!"

"Sure," said Jake. "But you're overthinking it again. Just have fun with it today. Basically we get to talk with people who drink strong coffee like we do, listen to Coldplay like we do, and enjoy a good sushi dinner like we do. God can overcome the differences that are there. He wants these people saved. So just be yourself."

"Yeah. You're right, I guess," Jen said, though not entirely convinced.

When Jenny and Jake got back to the hostel where they were all staying, Jun had just brought by some noodles for breakfast. Brian thanked him for the extra effort but said, "I'm going to run around the corner and grab an Egg McMuffin. I need something normal before I teach today." Brian didn't want to feel queasy before his first day of teaching. While some of the others ate breakfast with Jun, Brian reviewed his notes at McDonald's.

What Is Perseverance CQ?

Perseverance CQ refers to our level of interest, drive, and motivation to adapt cross-culturally. It's a traveler's robustness, courage, hardiness, and capability to persevere through cultural differences. A person high in perseverance CQ draws great satisfaction from being in new places and interacting with people from different cultures. A person low in perseverance CQ avoids engagement with the culture as a whole. Short-termers with low perseverance CQ hope to stay in comfortable hotels, interact primarily with their fellow teammates, and eat familiar foods. In contrast, short-termers with high perseverance CQ want to adapt to the new culture not only to do short-term missions well but also because they're genuinely interested in learning about life in a different place.

People high in perseverance CQ are internally motivated to learn about a new place. They want to ask the deeper questions which can only come through interpretive CQ. As they begin to observe some of the differences and some of the ways their own assumptions are challenged, if they're high in perseverance CQ, they don't run from facing those differences. Instead they persist in trying to adapt in light of their observations. They don't persevere through this process in isolation. They actively seek relationships with people who are culturally different. For these kinds of individuals, a short-term mission trip is just one of many opportunities in the course of a year when they will seek out cross-cultural experiences. The person with high perseverance CQ is always on the lookout for opportunities to understand different cultures and different ways of seeing the world.

Perseverance CQ is one of the most overlooked aspects of short-term missions. Knowledge and behavioral CQ are the elements of CQ where the most attention is usually given. Fortunately many short-term teams conduct extensive orientation, which includes researching some of the understanding necessary to make the trip meaningful. Many teams spend time talking about the importance of their actual behavior on the trip and remind one another about that during the trip. But little attention is given to the aspect of motivation when it comes to short-term missions, or for that matter, as it relates to cross-cultural interactions in general. "This component of adaptation is generally neglected or given little serious attention."[1]

Ironically, perseverance CQ is the most important aspect of selecting people for cross-cultural work, including short-term mission work. As we saw in chapter 3, the way one anticipates and is motivated to participate in a short-term project directly influences how the individual experiences the trip. Motivation shapes cross-cultural engagement more than anything else.

It's not enough to simply be motivated. Quite honestly we're not short on passion and zeal when it comes to short-term missions. We saw that in the things we explored earlier. Many of our short-term endeavors come from our confidence that they're biblical and because we love the adventure that accompanies them. More than anything else, we're motivated to do short-term missions because of the potential impact upon ourselves and others. All these motivators powerfully shape our assumptions about what should happen on the trip. The question lies in whether our motivations are accurate and healthy, which ties perseverance CQ back to the last two CQ elements we just talked about—knowledge and interpretive CQ. Is our understanding accurate, and are we remaining alert in order to interpret cues appropriately?

Perseverance CQ doesn't happen in a vacuum. Our levels of motivation are connected to the motivations of those with whom we travel, and most of all, to those closest to us. Throughout the past couple decades of Americans traveling and working abroad, a great deal of research has examined the role of one's family and friends in how an individual works cross-culturally. If you're really excited about going on an overseas assignment, but your spouse or kids aren't, that has a direct impact upon your level of motivation. If a close friend is on a trip with you and has little interest in really experiencing the culture, that immediately challenges your level of interest in engaging with the culture.

Motivation is also shaped by our cultural backgrounds. While we can't assume everyone from one place is more motivated than everyone from another place, it's important to understand the relationship between our cultural programming and how we're likely to score on perseverance CQ. For example, Americans typically have lower success rates adjusting to other cultures compared to many other ethnic groups. There are a number of reasons for this. One of the primary contributing factors for our poor adaptation cross-culturally comes from our individualistic orientation. We're programmed to pursue our own interests and "do our own thing." So the very idea that doing something beyond what we can see might immediately benefit us personally is counterintuitive. Furthermore, despite our espoused desire to learn from others, it's ingrained in us as Americans that we're the leaders of the world. With that mind-set comes a set of assumptions that make it more challenging to have a high level of motivation to truly adapt cross-culturally.

In similar fashion, as Americans, receiving positive feedback often motivates us. I've often been a bit paralyzed in working cross-culturally because I hear so little verbal feedback either for others or myself. However, in many cultural contexts, expressing positive feedback is seen as a form of humiliation and embarrassment, so more indirect feedback is preferable. All of these cultural dynamics play a part in understanding perseverance CQ.

In contrast, cultures that score low in individualism approach cross-cultural adaptation much differently. They're motivated most by what's good for the whole group. For example, McDonald's wasn't successful in using its "Employee of the Month" program in Nepal in the same way it uses it here. So in Nepal, McDonald's rotates the award among teams of employees rather than singling out an individual. To award a single individual would not only be demotivating but it would be humiliating for most Nepalese.[2]

One of the most important aspects of understanding perseverance CQ is our desire to adapt not only to the immediate task at hand but our interest in adapting to the culture as a whole. Typically, people who travel overseas to work, whether for business or missions, are motivated to do their work well. An American businesswoman wants to successfully run the branch office in Bangkok. The Chicago pastor training in Ghana wants to feel as if he's communicated the content well with the people being trained. However, the same individuals often demonstrate a much lower level of motivation for adjusting to the culture as a whole. The businessperson in Thailand might think a ride down the Chau Phraya River in a river taxi has little to do with how she runs the office; and the American pastor might think eating Ghanaian food has little influence on his teaching. The research demonstrates exactly the opposite. Our level of interest in connecting with the culture as a whole will directly shape how well we do our work in subtle but profound ways.

The same dynamics apply to short-term missions. Most short-term participants have low perseverance CQ when it comes to truly engaging in the life of a culture. We have a strong desire to complete the roof project and do it well. We want to reach as many kids as possible through the vacation Bible school program we're running, or we want to really help the pastors we're training. Those are noble and worthy forms of motivation, but by themselves, they aren't enough. In fact, too much interest and motivation to do our tasks well may impede our ability to actually engage with people there. We're inclined to be so focused upon our task that we miss out on some of the more important conversations and experiences we need. As a result, many of our short-term projects are done with a low level of perseverance CQ. We end up observing the novelties of a new place from afar rather than really immersing ourselves in the context. We look for familiar foods and crave a current copy of *USA Today* on our way to paint the wall, and so we miss a huge part of the experience.

Perseverance CQ goes beyond simply the excitement of traveling to a new place. It's the perseverance required when the novelty wears off and the differences start to chafe at us. Given its importance and the tendency to neglect to consider motivation, it's essential we consider a few ways to begin nurturing perseverance CQ.

Nurturing Perseverance CQ

Nurturing the desire and motivation to adapt cross-culturally is especially challenging when it involves a project as brief as ten days to two weeks. When expatriates move overseas for several years, they often have a much higher level of motivation to adapt because of the longevity of their tenure. However, there's often little interest in adapting to the culture by those who engage in short-term mission efforts. There are a number of ways to address this. Here are a few considerations.

Connect to Knowledge and Interpretive CQ

I've already stated several times that all four components of CQ are interdependent. It's important to especially point out the connection between knowledge CQ and interpretive CQ in how we motivate ourselves and others for short-term mission trips. There's plenty of passion and zeal for short-term missions so we don't need to do much to nurture that. The challenge is how we align our motivation with what we are growing to understand about a culture—both through knowledge and interpretive CQ.

For example, a highly energized, friendly American who takes a short-term trip to a high power-distance society (where leaders and followers keep their distance) will need to display his energy and excitement in light of what he should know about how that culture views status. Perhaps the short-termer thinks, *Forget about all these distinctions based upon the color of skin or money. I'm going to show these people we don't believe in that.* Imagine he meets a low-status cleaning lady, stops to talk with her, and then gives her a warm embrace as he walks away. His desire to love her just as she is, is commendable. However, she may miss entirely what he's trying to communicate because he violated his understanding about power distance. This may well be an area in which Christians need to be countercultural. However, he needs to understand that the cleaning lady might get a different message than he intended.

Sheer willpower to effectively connect cross-culturally and pure facts about cross-cultural differences are equally useless by themselves. Together they can play a powerful role in helping us effectively minister cross-culturally. High perseverance CQ helps us use our cross-cultural understanding to shape our behavior.

Furthermore if we seriously work on developing interpretive CQ, that kind of reflective and interpretive thought will lead to some unsettling things. As we begin to see some of the differences in how our minds are programmed, we begin to question things we've held to securely. However, when we lean into the tensions and uncertainty that come from facing our questions, we have the chance to deepen our perseverance CQ, which in turn leads to enhanced CQ as a whole. We grow in our tolerance of uncertainty and in learning to see things differently. Persevering through the hard work of seeking to understand, and stepping back to make sense of that, is directly connected to our level of perseverance in adapting cross-culturally.

Be Honest

In part 2 we encountered some convincing research that questions the impact of short-term missions upon both the goers and the receivers. While clearly that information needs to factor in to how we think about short-term missions, it is unlikely that short-term missions have no impact. On the other hand, we must use the research to temper the exaggerated ways we talk about the impact of short-term missions. One of the things we heard again and again as we saw the conflicting perspectives of American short-termers vis-à-vis national church members who received the short-termers was our exaggerated descriptions of what happens as a result of these trips.

Our motivation for short-term missions typically involves an overstated description of what happens in others and us. We talk about changing entire communities that don't look all that different after we leave. We describe the lifelong changes in us, including our commitments to pray more and give more, but within six to eight weeks, most of us are praying and giving about the same as before the trip.[3]

As I state more clearly in the final chapter, I think there are compelling, missional reasons to engage in short-term missions. But in our need to defend our trips to ourselves and our supporters, we must not overstate the influence of the trip—upon either us or those we serve. I have little trouble believing some kind of transformation occurs when we leave the comforts of home to spend life in an entirely different world for a couple weeks. Likewise, when a group of Mexicans host a group of Americans for a week, surely that makes some impact as well, just as my every encounter in life plays at least some role in who I am and how I view the world and God. However, can we get to the point of seeing our short-term mission trips as one of many life experiences that impact us and others? May we have the boldness to consider how we're doing them, and if our doing them in certain places and certain ways is the best way to serve.

As we begin to be more honest about the fact that short-term mission trips are simply another piece of thousands of experiences in our lives that change us, we'll be motivated in appropriate ways, which in turn will help us engage more effectively. Let's stop thinking about short-term missions as a service to perform and see them as another expression of a seamless life of missional living that includes giving and receiving. Let's think about them as a time when we're responsible to learn. When we're with brothers and sisters from another part of the world, let's spend less time thinking about how we can tell everyone back home what we did for them and more time finding out what they're truly facing and getting their perspective on how we can help them. Before we're sure that our time spent painting a wall is the best thing we can do, let's be willing to reconsider that. With high levels of unemployment in most of the places we visit, are we taking jobs away from people who need them when we do our building projects? There are probably times when it's appropriate to do a building project, but be willing to slow down and ask the question before jumping in.

This is really challenging because often the request to build the building or to come provide training comes from nationals themselves. I encounter this all the time. I frequently interact with majority world church leaders who request curriculum and resources developed in the West. I don't doubt they can make use of them, but part of my being honest about the true needs means sometimes challenging even the requests that come from our national brothers and sisters. The honesty we're after has to come from a broad perspective from what God's doing among his people all over the world, and continually learning what our role is in serving what God is doing. Sometimes we need to sacrifice our egos and say, "I'm not going to come train. I want to do whatever I can to help you train the material that's developed by your context for your context." Or we might need to say, "We're not going to build that. We're going to raise the money for you to employ your people to build it."

As we pursue this kind of honest questioning and motivating, we begin to move away from the drive-by mission trip mind-set. Accurate perspective on what can happen within others and us is the kind of honesty our supporters deserve, not to mention our brothers and sisters in Christ in the majority world church. This kind of honesty about what we are and aren't doing through short-term missions is an essential part of nurturing perseverance CQ. Over the long haul, we'll stay motivated far longer and persevere through much more cultural dissonance when we become honest about what we have to offer and what we have to gain.

Relevance

Few of us are motivated to do something if it feels irrelevant and disconnected from our lives. In order to be motivated to persevere through the challenges of cross-cultural work, we must see how they relate to our other goals. This is a basic rule of learning. We aren't motivated to learn about things that we perceive to be irrelevant to our needs. The mind-set is, "If I have to learn algebra, help me see why I'll ever need this!" Clearly this is the challenge as we seek to motivate others to think about cultural intelligence. We have to help them see how eating unfamiliar foods, sitting through services in a foreign language, and touring ancient temples is relevant to God's call on their lives. It's imperative that we frame our experiences as pertinent and related to the overall goals of our lives. As we move into the last chapter, we'll examine short-term missions from a "big picture" perspective in our lives and the life of the church.

The average short-term team won't see how eating at McDonald's could hinder their vacation Bible school program. Yet we need to see the subtle but profound connections between where we eat, where we stay, and how we interact and how we fulfill our mission tasks. Soak in the culture and set the tone for others traveling with you about the importance of doing so for your overall mission. Persevere through difficult interactions, try the foods and the language, continue the hard work of journaling, and seek to understand what's really going on beneath the surface of what you see. If you're leading a short-term mission trip, challenge your group members to soak in the culture as much as possible. Help them see how taking it all in can directly relate to fulfilling your mission—both your short-term mission and your lifelong calling to extend the redemptive mission of God.

Back to Shanghai

Brian had a great day. While at numerous times he struggled to feel proficient in teaching English to the students in his group, he was still energized. He'd been preparing for this for years! Interacting with the students in the classroom was what he came to do. At last, he felt the trip was worth it.

The team got together to debrief their first day of teaching. Jake, the infamous storyteller of the group, shared a few of his greatest blunders. Jenny, the ever-reflective one, bombarded Jun with questions: "Why won't anyone respond when I ask the group a question? Will I offend them if I ask them not to call me Miss Gilmore? Some of them are older than me! Should I try to make things more participatory or is it better for me to use the lecture-style that they seem more comfortable with? Or am I right in assuming they're more comfortable with lecture?" For each of Jun's responses, Sarah, the cross-cultural expert, had her own two cents to throw in.

Brian was quickly losing heart. He said, "Hey, this is fun and all, you guys, but I need a hazelnut latte! Anyone want to join me at Starbucks around the corner?"

Jun said, "Oh, I'm so sorry. I don't know if we have time right now, Brian. Some of the university students have invited you to join them at Yuyuan Garden for a while. Yuyuan Garden is said to be part of the Ming Dynasty. It's a peaceful, beautiful place right in the heart of the city, and a group of my students asked if you'll be their guests there tonight for a while."

Brian asked, "Can I ask what 'a while' means? Are we talking an hour or so or the entire evening?"

Jun said, "Don't worry about that. We'll just go for a while and see how you like it."

"Wow, that sounds really great," Brian continued. "My only concern is I really need to spend some time preparing for class tomorrow." Inside, Brian was thinking, *I don't need to hang out in some ancient garden! I'm not here to be a tourist. I want to be on top of my game to teach tomorrow.*

You can see what's happening here. Brian is the epitome of the conscientious short-termer who wants to perform his task with excellence. He's to be affirmed for that. He demonstrates some good knowledge CQ in knowing that teaching isn't something that can be done cross-culturally by just winging it. Subconsciously, if not consciously, Brian appears to have some interpretive CQ too. He received some cues today as he was teaching, and he wants to use those to reframe the way he teaches tomorrow.

Unfortunately Brian doesn't understand that one of the things that might help him most tomorrow is spending time with a group of Chinese peers tonight in a place they've invited him to come. A trip to the garden probably won't directly translate into teaching material for tomorrow; however, without Brian even knowing how, persevering through cultural experiences like this, and most of all, spending time with these local students, will be far more important to how he continues to engage with his own students the next couple weeks than he can imagine. Eating local food, walking down Nanjing Road, and lingering in Yuyuan Garden is probably what Brian needs far more right now to enhance his cultural intelligence than spending a couple hours reviewing his notes for tomorrow.

Actions Speak Louder than Words

Behavioral CQ

Jun flagged down a couple taxis to get everyone over to Yuyuan Garden. Jake and Jun ended up in the same taxi together, so Jake used it as a chance to get some feedback from Jun. "So, Jun. How's it going, bro? Are we doing okay? Are you happy with the team?"

"Everything is okay," said Jun. "It's fine."

"Well what's that supposed to mean?" asked Jake. "That's a very noncommittal answer—. 'Okay'? 'Fine'? C'mon, bud. Shoot straight with me. How do you feel the team is doing?"

"It's okay, Jake. We will talk about it." Jun immediately started pointing out the Chongqing Harbor where the Yangtze and Jialing Rivers meet.

Jake was a little frustrated by Jun's nondescriptive feedback, but he decided not to push it any further. Instead he feigned interest in the places Jun pointed out along the way.

Meanwhile Mandy, one of the other team members, struck up a conversation with her taxi driver. His English impressed her. It turns out he spent several years in Hong Kong. Knowing the prevalence of the British influence in Hong Kong, Mandy purposely used the hard "o" when she said the word *process*. She had some Canadian friends who always said it that way. She said words like *library* really fast, as she had often heard Brits do. She referred to it as the "libree." As Jenny and Brian listened to her talk with the taxi driver, they began to laugh as she forced British pronunciations of English words.

Jenny, the ever-reflective one, wondered what Mandy was doing. *Is that really more effective than just speaking English the way we typically speak it? I wonder if it sounds as forced to this driver as it does to me.* Was Mandy's behavior a good demonstration of cultural intelligence? Is that what it looks like to be high in behavioral CQ?

What Is Behavioral CQ?

Behavioral CQ is the extent to which we change our verbal and nonverbal actions when interacting cross-culturally. Everything from how fast we talk to what we talk about is part of behavioral CQ. Cultural taboos such as pointing or talking with our hands in our pockets are some of the endless actions included in observing behavioral CQ. Behavioral CQ is being sensitive and appropriate with our actions and behavior as we engage in a new culture. Again the point isn't to act as chameleons wherever we go. Rather, in an attempt to empathetically relate to our fellow human beings, we want to learn how to interact in meaningful and appropriate ways.

The other three elements of cultural intelligence are vitally important for all the reasons we've just explored. At the end of the day, however, our cultural intelligence and, more importantly, our short-term mission endeavors, will be measured by our behavior. The things we actually say and do and the ways we go about our work become the litmus test for whether we're doing short-term missions with cultural intelligence. As we'll see shortly, the other elements are essential in nurturing behavioral CQ, but cultural intelligence is not just a mind game of gathering information, interpreting cues, and having the right motivation. Eventually we must act. Our ability to actually draw upon all the other CQ factors and act appropriately is behavioral CQ.

The biggest problems for most short-term mission teams are not technical or administrative. The biggest challenges lie in communication, misunderstanding, personality conflicts, poor leadership, and bad teamwork. These are all parts of behavioral CQ. The difference between short-term trips done with behavioral CQ as compared to those without is significant. Short-term mission trips without behavioral CQ look more like a typical tourist experience where the tour group sticks together as a group of outsiders, stays in cushy places, seldom veers into the local cuisine, and views the culture as a sporting event rather than actually playing the game.

An important part of behavioral CQ is seeing the ways the same behaviors can have different meanings in different places. Behaviors such as laughing, shouting, smiling, and talking quietly are some universal behaviors we share as humans. However, culture programs our minds to interpret those behaviors differently. Smiling is expected upon certain occasions and assumed to mean certain things in one place, but has entirely different uses elsewhere. Nudity is crude in public and intimate in private for most Americans, but has very different associative meanings in many tribal cultures. Students sitting still and nodding their heads can mean something entirely different in one culture as compared to the next.

An individual with high behavioral CQ is not necessarily someone who learns to master all the unique habits and behaviors of every culture visited. That's next to impossible, especially during brief immersions like short-term mission trips. Instead, flexibility and adjustment is the crucial competency that accompanies behavioral CQ. A person high in behavioral CQ will use nonverbal cues as a "silent language" to learn in various places, and will be careful not to quickly assign meanings. The goal is reducing misunderstanding more than it is mimicking others' behavior.

Behaving in a way that's culturally intelligent is clearly one of those "easier said than done" things. For years I've understood theoretically that it's not uncommon for men in many cultures to hold hands with other men, without it meaning anything beyond a display of friendship. I've often explained this phenomenon to other people as a clear example of our need to beware of making quick judgments based on the same behavior in our culture. It was another whole thing, however, when I was walking down the streets of Chiang Rai, Thailand, and John, an Akha man, slipped his hand around my waist. He put his hand in my left rear pocket as a high school boyfriend might do with his American girlfriend. He left it there as we walked for several blocks. I desperately wanted to pull away. It was one thing to read about it in a sterile environment back home; it was quite another to experience it while walking through the streets of Chiang Rai. So what does it look like for us to actually nurture CQ in our actions?

Nurturing Behavioral CQ

There are more resources devoted to helping us act appropriately when we travel cross-culturally than for any other CQ component. Several authors give us a lot of helpful information about the kinds of gifts to avoid giving. We're told how to entertain, gestures to avoid, how to exchange business cards, and the kinds of greetings to use. "Don't point. Never pay with your left hand. Kiss both cheeks. Don't hug. Be sure to use her formal title." The lists are endless. If we move to a culture for several years, it's fathomable that we might be able to master these behaviors, but what does it look like when we move in and out of different cultures all the time? There are several things to consider in nurturing behavioral CQ.

Seeing Behavioral CQ as the Outcome

At the risk of being redundant, the most important way to nurture behavioral CQ is to nurture the other three CQ elements—knowledge, interpretive, and perseverance CQ. This is the irony. The success of our short-term projects is judged mostly by our behavior. Our actions demonstrate most clearly whether or not we're culturally intelligent. However, trying to change our behavior itself is the least effective way of nurturing CQ. Our actions are so ingrained into our habits that it takes far more than a book or several training sessions to teach us behavioral CQ.

However, as we nurture the other aspects of CQ, they have inevitable implications on how we act. In a sense behavioral CQ is the outcome of the other three factors of CQ. For example, as we use knowledge CQ to understand the different ways cultures approach power distance, it will begin to inform how we interact with people of different status. Interpretive CQ will help us tune in to the cues coming from our interactions and organize those cues within our growing sense of cultural intelligence as a whole. However, only as we persevere through the hard work of these cross-cultural interactions as measured through perseverance CQ will we actually see our changing perspectives result in adaptive behavior.

As described in the paragraphs below, some behaviors can be modified and manipulated, but most of our energy should be placed on the other three facets of CQ. Behavioral CQ is perhaps the most helpful way to expose our need for cultural intelligence. As we seek to actually change our behavior, we don't have access to each other's thoughts, feelings, or motivation. We can rely only on what we see and hear in other's verbal, vocal, facial, and other bodily expressions. Nurturing our knowledge, interpretive, and perseverance CQ addresses those realities.

Practice

Second to continuing the hard work of nurturing the other areas of CQ, we can attempt to learn some basic habits and make them part of our behavioral repertoire. For example, because people in so many places where I travel consider the left hand an offensive part of the body, even when I'm home, I avoid handing something to someone with my left hand. Obviously, 99 percent of the people with whom I interact in the United States don't give a second thought to whether they receive my change at the cash register from my right hand or my left hand. However, I want it to be second nature for me to use my right hand to avoid offending an Arab acquaintance.

I speak very fast, especially when I teach or preach. This is another area where I have to practice—slowing down. Frankly, my American audiences also would be happy if I'd chill a bit when I speak. When I speak overseas, I often do so with people who speak English as a second language or where an interpreter is translating on my behalf. Because my rate of speech is so ingrained in how I communicate, I work to slow down my public speaking. In such behavioral areas I can purposely practice to nurture my behavioral CQ. Practice. Practice. Practice.

Adaptability

Some of us are complete naturals at interacting with people—even if they're complete strangers. We find it easy to initiate conversations, listen to others, and bring other people into the conversation. Others struggle desperately to master a conversation. Having a natural ability socially can be a real help cross-culturally, but we must beware of thinking we can rely on those skills alone when interacting with someone from a different cultural background. Often new social skills need to be developed. This is one of many reasons why the most important trait to develop for behavioral CQ is adaptability.

As we learn to become adaptable and flexible, we'll gain the behavioral CQ needed to interact with unique individuals and situations. The challenge lies in gaining some general skills of adaptability so that we can adapt instantly to specific people, cultures, and circumstances. "Cross-cultural skills are not fixed routines but flexible abilities that can—with the guidance of mindfulness—be modified to meet new or changing conditions."[1] The challenge is to extend the range or repertoire of skilled behaviors needed in different places and knowing how to use each one. The skilled routines we master in one culture might be counterproductive in another, to the extent that we have to "unlearn" them in a new situation. Again, this is why adaptability is a crucial skill needed to nurture behavioral CQ.

As in several of these areas, some cultures program individuals to be better at this than others. For example, cultures that feel less threatened by uncertainty—such as Singaporeans, Brits, and Jamaicans—typically achieve behavioral CQ more easily. In addition, learning to be adaptable is directly connected to our interpretive CQ. It's a part of the interpretive process where we learn to read cues and change our plans based upon what seems to work and what doesn't. Having a plan so we don't fly by the seat of our pants is an integral part of interacting with behavioral CQ, but just as essential is the process of holding to those plans loosely and being willing to toss them in a split second when necessary.

Cross-cultural experiences are one of the greatest ways to grow our ability to be adaptable. As we gain understanding about cultural dynamics, use that knowledge to reframe our assumptions, and persevere through the continual challenges confronting us in cross-cultural communication and interaction, we begin to behave more appropriately.

Behavioral Training

Most of the cross-cultural training tools developed relate closely to the knowledge and behavioral dimensions of cultural intelligence. General training to aid short-term participants in the overall activity of cross-cultural behavior is helpful, as is training developed for work in specific places. The key challenge lies at the point of integration, where we can begin to move more freely from one place to another. Training that works on developing adaptability skills can help us move with greater ease in and out of different places without resorting to oversimplification.

One of the most effective ways to train yourself and your short-term team in behavioral CQ is exposure to uncomfortable situations. For example, you could begin having a conversation about the challenges of behavioral CQ by walking up to a friend and purposely violating his personal space. Keep within two inches of his face, and as he backs away from you, keep moving with him. Have the whole group try this with each other. Or suddenly put your hand on your friend's shoulder and leave it there as you talk. Or talk in a way that eliminates nonverbal expressions as much as possible. Or choose an unusual, unfamiliar food and insist that everyone eat it. These kinds of experiences help to train behavioral CQ. More than anything, they help reveal the need for CQ as a whole.

It's easy to speak confidently about our ability to act appropriately, but when we become uncomfortable, it's another whole thing. As a result, one of the most significant times for doing behavioral "training" is when we first enter a new culture and when we first return home. These are our most pivotal learning times. The first impressions and the immediate dissonance experienced both in leaving home and coming back are filled with opportunities for learning adaptability. Be sure to check out the cross-cultural training resources listed in the appendix for more guidance on behavioral training.

Back to Shanghai

Jake is a natural conversationalist. He can talk to complete strangers on the street and put them at ease. The highly relational context of Mexico where he grew up has really helped him in being a natural leader and networker most anywhere he's been. So far, however, he doesn't seem to have really connected with Jun. In particular he violated the social practices of Chinese culture when he asked Jun for a direct evaluation and assessment in the midst of a very informal setting—riding in a taxi. Jun just wasn't going to go there. He gave Jake a very nebulous response. Jake knew what it would mean if he evaluated a group by saying, "It's okay" or "It's fine." That would be code language for, "I'm not very impressed."

Meanwhile Mandy wants so hard to speak appropriately that she's trying to incorporate British-style English into her vocabulary rather than just saying words like *process* and *library* as an American would. What she doesn't realize, however, is that her attempts at acting appropriately might in fact have exactly the opposite effect from what she seeks. The taxi driver could easily be insulted. Why does Mandy think he isn't smart enough to figure out what she means when she pronounces words the way she typically would? Inevitably the taxi driver has seen lots of American television and movies throughout his years in Hong Kong and now in Shanghai. Does he really need Mandy to force herself to pronounce words differently?

Actions speak louder than words. This cliché, though overused, really applies here. Most of the short-term participants I've studied said the right things before going cross-culturally. They demonstrated a desire to learn, they realized they might come off as loud and brash, and they were well aware of their shortcomings when it comes to cross-cultural work. Yet when they actually went on their trips, much of their behavior didn't line up with what they had said.

Our tendency is to use all our energy trying to change behavior, but we can't possibly anticipate the endless situations and encounters that will arise. So the full-orbed approach of CQ is essential to getting our actions to speak a message that lines up with the glory of God.

The Heart of the Matter

Shema

Perhaps you're thinking, "What's the point? Cultural intelligence, interpretive CQ, power distance—does it have to be so complicated? I just want to go love people in Romania!"

Or maybe you're thinking, "Forget it! You've convinced me so many problems occur with short-term missions that I'm going to boycott the whole deal."

I hope you don't come to either conclusion. I understand the tension. Surely we don't want to make missions so complicated that you need a PhD in intercultural studies to succeed, but neither do we want to easily explain away the many downfalls of past mistakes.

At the end of the day, cultural intelligence—serving with eyes wide open—helps us do what we were created to do—extend the mission of God. At the very core of being human is the task of missions. In my mind, mission isn't something that started after Adam and Eve sinned, and it's not just about getting souls saved. It's about living in light of our position as image bearers of God. Mission—short-term, long-term, overseas, next-door—is about giving people a living picture of who God is, what he cares about, and how he acts. Mission is what Adam and Eve were created and called by God to do long before sin entered the picture.

Mission Began with Adam and Eve

Paul is often called the first missionary. Others label the disciples as the first missionaries, and still others go as far back as Abraham. However, I prefer to go all the way back to Adam and Eve. They were the first humans called by God to live out the mission of reflecting his glory. Long before sin corrupted the earth, ages before churches painted Matthew 28 on banners for their mission conferences, God called Adam and Eve to be his missional agents. Men and women are the creatures he created to act on his behalf in the world.

Mission is rooted in creation. It's not simply a corrective to sin. It's what God created us to do as human beings. God called Adam and Eve to reflect his glory by acting on his behalf with all of creation. They were to care for the animals and the garden as God would. They were to creatively develop their surroundings. God told them to be fruitful and multiply and to show their children and grandchildren who he is and what he cares about. Adam and Eve were to reflect the glory of God with every word and deed. They were called upon by God to be the priests over all creation—to represent God to creation and represent creation to God.

Though Adam and Eve failed at their mission, God's call on his people to be his missional agents continued. The nation of Israel was created by God to be a priestly nation to the other nations. They were to give the other nations a picture of what a group of people obeying God looked like. Along with the privileges of being the favored nation, Israel was called to be the nation that would bless other nations. They were to act on God's behalf among the other nations.

Though Israel failed, God's call on his people to be agents continued. He divided the priestly nation into twelve tribes, and the Levitical tribe became the priestly tribe. Notice the narrowing impact to which God was calling his people. Adam and Eve were given a priestly role among all creation, Israel to the rest of the nations, and Aaron and his sons to the nation of Israel, to intercede on their behalf with God. As they failed in accurately reflecting who God is, their missional impact kept getting smaller and smaller.[1]

The Levitical priests also failed in their missional calling, but God's redemptive plan continued. Jesus, the second Adam, came as the perfect priest and sacrifice all in one. God became one of us, in part, so that we could see how he intended for us to live. He was the epitome of "cultural intelligence" by giving us the most accessible and understandable picture of how he intended for us to live by becoming a human himself. From that long history of God calling his people to be his agents, Jesus declares, "Go and make disciples of *all* nations" (Matt. 28:19, emphasis mine). Jesus reextends our broad missional calling to all the nations. We're called to extend God's reign among people everywhere.

Jesus's disciples obeyed the Great Commission by establishing the church. Peter refers to the church as the "priesthood" of believers (1 Peter 2:9). As part of the church, we're to live out the priestly mission that has been upon the people of God throughout history. Just as Adam and Eve, Israel, and the disciples were called to extend God's reign, so also are we. Short-term mission trips are a way for us to join with a long legacy of God's people in making him known to all the world.[2]

God has continually called us as his people to be engaged in mission. We don't have the prerogative of either extreme: "Who cares about all that CQ stuff; I just want to go serve!" or "I'm going to boycott the whole mission thing. There's too much baggage." Missions is who and what we're created to be and do—together. So we must figure out how to keep improving our obedience to God's calling upon us.

If missions is what we were created to do, and if we're to be the physical presence of Christ in the world, then working on how to best embody him to the world should be of prime importance—that's the essence of cultural intelligence. For our purposes, CQ is more than a trendy model for talking about cross-cultural work. It's a way to enhance how we live out our eternal mission as people—to reflect God's glory to the world. It's more than just a tool for short-term mission trips. It's a pathway for helping us live out our mission as we encounter people from different cultures in a growing number of encounters every day—at the airport, at school, at work, on the phone, in the grocery store, and online.

What Matters Most?

As we live out Christ's presence in the world, it's worth reminding ourselves what Jesus considered to be the most important commandment: "Love God, love others." Everything else rises and falls on this.

This was Jesus's reply when the teacher of the law asked him, "Jesus, which is the greatest commandment in the Law?" (Matt. 22:36). Jesus's response wasn't random. He quoted something he had been reciting since his childhood—a portion of the Shema from the Old Testament. *Shema* means "to listen" or "to hear." To the Jew, the Shema was as familiar as the song "Jesus Loves Me" is to many of us today. The Shema was one of those phrases children recited when they were young, and they never forgot it.

Jesus's reference to the Shema helps us live out mission— whether in our everyday lives back home or during a two-week mission trip. He brings us back to the focus of what God's people were called to do all throughout the Old Testament. For several centuries, day after day, year after year, the people of God recited the Shema as a continual reminder of what mattered most as they lived out their mission. The Shema was to be embraced in their hearts, impressed upon their children, and declared to all who encountered them both in word and deed (Deuteronomy 6).

This daily practice of reciting the Shema again and again and again continued during Jesus's day. He grew up reciting it with Mary and Joseph at home and in the nearby synagogues. This was what followers of God declared every day during Jesus's childhood as a way to firmly acknowledge their allegiance to God alone. To recite Shema was to wholeheartedly accept the kingdom of God in their lives.

Paul continued to declare the centrality of the Shema to living out the mission of God. Paul frequently referenced the priorities of loving God and loving others as he ministered for several decades after Jesus ascended to heaven. All his letters included both emphases.

The whole purpose of enhancing our cultural intelligence is to use it as a way to get better at loving God and loving others. As we understand the people God has made in cultures all over the world, we're drawn to worship him. As we persevere through the challenges that come with interacting cross-culturally, we demonstrate a love that reflects God's glory. As we behave in ways that set others at ease and respect their differences, we give people glimpses of Jesus. That's why CQ is so vital. It's not about simply being more successful at cross-cultural work; it's a way to move us forward in living missionally.

As soon as we lose sight of the Shema, we risk doing short-term missions for ourselves rather than for the sake of those we're serving—or God. Self-serving missions can be described as "Christian 'parachuting,' a decontextualized 'dropping in' to a needy situation just long enough to distribute beneficial goods that sometimes places unwanted stress on a beleaguered community."[3] These kinds of so-called mission trips are more like sightseeing than genuine service and ministry to a group of people. We cannot truly serve those we do not know and love. However, as we enter into deep relationship with those we serve, we, in a small way like Jesus, take on other's burdens as our own and through authentic relationships, begin to truly lay down our lives so that those we serve might encounter the life of Jesus.[4]

Love for people and love for God has to drive our short-term mission work. That will happen only as short-term mission experiences become part of a lifelong journey of seeking to love people cross-culturally, whenever and wherever we encounter them.

We've covered a lot of ground in our journey together. My hope is that you won't be paralyzed from engaging missionally in cross-cultural settings because of the many pitfalls exposed. Instead, continue to pursue cross-cultural opportunities to live out God's mission and do so with your eyes wide open. I want to conclude by reviewing several things to consider, as we serve with eyes wide open.

Ten Starting Points for Doing Short-Term Missions with Cultural Intelligence

1. God's a Lot Bigger than Your Short-Term Mission Trip

God's sovereignty above and beyond our mission trips should be a word of encouragement to some. Others need to hear that reality as a word of caution. Our American sense of urgency can cause us to think God's work around the world is entirely dependent upon our short-term mission projects and us. He's graciously allowed us to be part of how he extends his reign around the world, but he's using countless others as well. When we're discouraged, may we be reminded that God has had thousands of years of turning our most feeble attempts at living out his mission into beautiful reflections of his glory. When we're tempted to overstate our role, may we be reminded that only God can turn a heart of stone into a heart of flesh. Only God can use a group of twenty people holding Romanian babies to be part of what gives those babies a real-life experience with Jesus. In the words of Jonathan Edwards, at the end of the day, "God's work of power and grace will not be thwarted by our great many errors and sin."[5]

2. Stop Petting the Poor

Whenever possible, find a way to connect short-term projects to long-term, interdependent relationships. Dropping into a food shelter once a year at Thanksgiving or making random mission trips that get more and more stamps into our passports doesn't keep the Shema at the forefront of missions. To love people is to get involved in their lives. That's messy and complicated. Let's persevere through the hard work of hanging in there with the same group of people rather than blowing in and out of a lot of different places. When you go, sit down with people and hear their stories. Share your story—not just the shiny, testimony-material parts of your story. Share the parts that reveal your weakness.

The American church has things to share. The majority world church has things to share. The American church has needs. The majority world church has needs. Let's move beyond demeaning relationships that put us in positions of power and move toward interdependent, loving relationships where we meet one another's needs.

Here's what some African church leaders said when asked what they wanted most to say to American churches: "Please raise our dignity before the Christians and citizens of North America. We are not naive, backward, and ignorant black people. Instead we are your brothers and sisters in the family of God who are seeking to be faithful to his calling on our lives."

Initiatives like the one led by Chip Huber at Wheaton Academy give us a positive example of short-term missions done with a heart to benefit both the goers and the receivers. Huber describes the long-term relationship Wheaton Academy high school students have been developing with some of the Zamtran people in Zambia. It's a great picture of affluent, Chicago suburbanites engaging in mission *with* passionate, prayer-dependent Zambians. The Chicago students sacrificed time and money to raise more than $225,000 to battle AIDS among the Zamtran people; Zamtran believers sacrificed time and money to host the American students and taught them what it means to sacrificially pray. There are countless stories about how the Zamtrans blessed the Americans and the Americans blessed the Zamtrans. Together they discerned before God what it looked like to be a blessing among the nations, particularly among AIDS victims and their families.[6] There are many other examples of how long-term commitments to do mission interdependently and cross-culturally are extending the reign of God.

3. Be Yourself

The tension of all we've considered throughout this journey is to understand cross-cultural differences enough to begin to adapt and act appropriately without trying to be someone we aren't. *Serving with eyes wide open means seeing yourself and others in a new light and making appropriate changes to who you are and how you relate.* But it's not about trying to be like whomever you're with. Sometimes Americans react to the criticisms of majority world pastors by bashing all that's American. It can be tempting to deprecate everything "Western" as a way to gain credibility with non-Westerners, but that's inauthentic and an overreaction. There are some wonderful things about being Westerners and Americans, and while we have plenty to redeem in our culture, the point is not to run from the culture of which we're a part.

4. Seek to Understand

Prepare for your short-term trip by enhancing your knowledge CQ. Spend time learning about the cultural differences you'll encounter in the specific place where you're going. If possible, talk with others who have been where you're going, and best of all, interact with people from the culture itself. Use your short-term trip as a way to grow your overall understanding of cross-cultural differences. Use your growing understanding to give you an enhanced perspective on what occurs in cross-cultural situations without having a Sarah-like know-it-all approach.

5. On Second Thought—Think Again!

Question your assumptions. Question your assumptions. Question your assumptions. If this book has done nothing else, I hope it's played a part in opening your eyes to rethink your assumptions about short-term work. Interpretive CQ sounds really technical, but it's simply slowing down our activity long enough to step back and look at what's going on below the surface. Promise me you'll work on this during your next short-term trip. Practice it when you encounter someone from another culture in the next week or so. When you're inclined to make an assumption about that person, or hear someone else do so, stop and rethink whether it's an accurate assumption. Don't be too quick to jump to conclusions. Turn off the mental "cruise control."

Question your assumptions about why we we're doing mission trips in the first place (motivation). Question your assumptions about what's urgent and what isn't (urgency). Question your assumptions about how much the people you're going to encounter are like you (common ground). Question your assumptions about what's biblical (the Bible). Question your assumptions about how happy people are who make two dollars a day (money). Last but not least, please, please, please question your assumptions when you begin to quickly jump to either/or categories (simplicity). We'll make a lot of strides in embodying an accurate picture of Jesus when we step back and question our assumptions.

6. Try, Try Again

On the other hand, as you question, question, question, don't be so paralyzed that you remain in a never-ending cycle of contemplative reflection. Persevere through the conflicting perspectives you begin to observe by using perseverance CQ. I've been in cross-cultural settings where I have so overapologized for my American perspective while teaching that it became laborious for my students. I understated the value I could bring by saying I was merely there to facilitate discussion, to which my host privately countered, "We did not bring you all the way here just to facilitate our discussion. Teach!" We need to keep our awareness on high alert as we seek to gather and interpret cues and acknowledge our limitations up front, given our cultural programming. Then we need to teach with conviction and passion. Don't allow the challenges of cross-cultural difference make you so overly tentative and apologetic that you come off as timid and uncertain.

Without question, my hardest weeks of work are those I spend when I'm in a new place trying to navigate a whole new set of cultural values and assumptions. Cross-cultural work is not for the weary. The excitement of new sights and sounds wears off pretty quickly. But as we persevere through the inevitable conflict and dissonance, some of the greatest rewards for seeing ourselves, others, and God in renewed ways come through cross-cultural interaction and work.

7. Actions Speak Louder than Words

Eventually we must move beyond conceptualizing cross-cultural work and go for it through behavioral CQ. Mistakes are inevitable. Use your actions as a way to assess whether you're spending enough time in the other three dimensions of CQ, since those three are the best ways to enhance behavioral CQ. Few things will help you grow in those areas like actually encountering people and lifestyles in a different setting. I teach intercultural studies at a seminary, but I'm well aware that the classroom content can only do so much to enhance our students' cultural intelligence. There's no substitute for immersing them in actual cross-cultural situations.

If you're part of a group experience on a short-term team, be sure to allow regular time throughout the experience to process what's occurring by way of intercultural behavior. Find someone from the culture, preferably your host, to be a "cultural interpreter" for you. Don't just spend all your time with your fellow teammates or with Western missionaries. Finally, don't miss out on the value of the lessons that can be learned after returning home. Commit to investing in something more than a picture-sharing party. Find some ongoing ways to process the lessons learned as a way to enhance your behavioral CQ in future interactions cross-culturally. Read this book again after you come home. See how your perspective has changed since the first time you read it.

8. Give Up Trying to See Who's In and Who's Out

Obviously, sharing Christ with people is a core part of most short-term mission projects—whether through verbal presentations of the gospel or projects that tangibly embody elements of the gospel, such as medical clinics or relief work. While taking our missional calling seriously, we need to be freed from trying to figure out who's "in" as a member of the people of God and who's "out." I'm not suggesting we go easy on calling people to follow Jesus. Every one of our encounters, every day, should include a call to our fellow human beings to follow Christ—whether the call comes implicitly or explicitly.

However, we expend needless energy when we obsess over figuring out whether someone is "in" the Christian faith or not. I often talk with short-termers who are confused about which religions they should consider "close enough" to our faith that they can assume people in that religion are genuine believers. On the other hand, they want a list of the religions wherein any of its followers are "out." I'm really not interested in going there because it's far too risky for me to think I can ever know God's final judgment on another person. In the words of missiologist

Leslie Newbigin, "I do not claim to know in advance [a person's] ultimate destiny. I meet the person simply as a witness, as one who has been laid hold of by [Christ] and placed in a position where I can only point to Jesus as the one who can make sense of the whole human situation that [we share] as human beings."[7] I'm to faithfully love God and love others and leave up to God what only he can do—rescue their souls.

9. Incorporate Short-Term Missions as Part of Your Seamless Missional Journey

Serving with eyes wide open means not only asking the deeper, reflective questions evoked by interpretive CQ but also placing them within the full scope of our lives as yet another way of living out our missional calling. We better not reduce the priesthood of believers or our obedience to the Great Commission to short-term missions. If we do, most of us get to live out our missional calling to the nations only a couple weeks a year at best, maybe only once in a lifetime, and for people like my parents—never! Short-term missions can be part of the Great Commission and of living out our priestly role—*part* of it!

Don't go running overseas to do something you aren't already doing in your own neighborhood. If you want to fight for justice in the brothels of Cambodia, start by being an agent of justice in your home and at work. If you want to share Jesus with children in a Romanian orphanage, don't neglect the children playing at the park around the corner from your house. If you have a heart to use your business skills to help people in Uzbekistan create wealth, think about how your business practices in your suburban office have global implications.

I could go on and on. Teachers bring about educational reform, computer wizards develop software that serves people in places around the world, and musicians compose pieces that reflect God's glory—all are part of living out our missional calling in an increasingly multicultural world. Short-term missions is just another opportunity for us to live out what we need to be living 24/7 wherever we are.

As we've seen many times throughout the last few chapters, CQ is not something we master before our next mission trip.

It's a lifelong journey of wrestling with what it means to use our finances, our gifts, our connections, and our time to extend God's reign among all the nations. As we grow in our CQ, our short-term mission trips will more effectively be part of God's work in the world and will help us more effectively live out God's mission seamlessly—whether we're in a cubicle in Midwest America or swinging a hammer in Namibia.[8]

10. Love God, Love Others

More than anything else, "'Love the Lord your God with all your heart and with all your soul and with all your mind.' This is the first and greatest commandment. And the second is like it: 'Love your neighbor as yourself'" (Matt. 22:37–39).

When you get up and when you go to sleep—love God, love others. When you travel on vacation and when you travel as part of a mission team—love God, love others. When you encounter an immigrant and when you overhear a foreign language—love God, love others. The essence of serving with eyes wide open is gaining cultural intelligence in order to more effectively reflect God to people who are culturally different from you.

Conclusion

Most of what we've learned on our journey through this book is common to human nature. It's not unique to Americans. There are specific ways it gets played out by us as Americans, but we're all inclined toward a self-orientation that defines everything related to "us." However, my desire has been to speak directly to the ways our human nature demonstrates itself in our cross-cultural encounters as Americans. How does our lack of cultural intelligence diminish our attempts to love God and love others? That's the heart of the matter.

Open your eyes. Can you see what you missed before? The challenges for doing short-term missions well are huge. But they pale with the guarantee that God *will* call people to himself from every nation, tribe, language, and people group. I wrote this book because I want to change the way we think about short-term missions. Actually, I want more than that. I want to change the way we think about missions as a whole. At face value, just changing how we think might seem like an easy and rather unimpressive goal. However, changing the way we view the world and our role in it is anything but easy and I'm convinced the results will be revolutionary. Don't get me wrong; I'm not saying we just need more information. We've never had more information at our fingertips, but information about cross-cultural differences by itself isn't likely to be revolutionary. However, as we critically reflect on that information and use it to help us interpret our cross-cultural experiences, and draw upon the Holy Spirit to gain the perseverance needed to translate a new way of thinking into how we act cross-culturally, we'll see short-term missions in a whole new light. More important, we'll begin to see and thus live out missions in a much more culturally intelligent way.

We began in chapter 1 with a sobering description of the needs of the world. Your short-term mission trip to Mexico next summer might seem like an insignificant drop in the sea of these needs. But as you see your trip connected with the burgeoning growth of the Christian church throughout Latin America, and connected with your desire to love God and love others the fifty weeks of the year when you're not in Mexico, and connected to what God has been doing for several millennia through his people all over the world, your trip, when done with CQ, can be another tangible expression of God completing his worldwide revolution through people like you and me.

Open your eyes. Can you see it? There's a worldwide revolution going on among God's people and there has been ever since Adam and Eve. Despite the countless failures of God's people, God's reign continues to be extended all over the world. The church of Jesus Christ is growing faster than ever before. When we're part of the people of God, we're part of a worldwide revolution that can never be stopped. We don't do short-term missions because we're shamed into it or because we're looking for something to do over spring break. It's part of joining God in the worldwide revolution he's unfolding in places everywhere. Never before has Revelation 7:9 seemed more viable. Can you see it? Can you see what John saw? Stranded out on the remote island of Patmos, the apostle John said, "There before me was a great multitude that no one could count, from every nation, tribe, people and language, standing before the throne and in front of the Lamb"

(Rev. 7:9). It's going to happen. People from *every* nation will gather at the feet of Jesus, worshiping him. We get to be part of making that happen, along with the rest of God's people spread across the globe.

I pray you'll take the challenge to embark on a lifelong journey of cultural intelligence so that you might love others better, and in turn, grow in your love for the Father. May the world never look the same as a result of your resolve to serve with eyes wide open.

Appendix

Recommended Resources

Practical Trip-Planning Guides

These tools are extremely practical in planning the logistics of your trip, including checklists, safety guidelines, getting the right documents together, and so on.

Forward, David C. *The Essential Guide for the Short-Term Mission Trip*. Chicago: Moody, 1998.
Stiles, J. Mack, and Leanne Stiles. *Mack and Leeann's Guide to Short-term Mission*. Downers Grove, IL: InterVarsity, 2000.

Devotional

These workbooks are good tools to use by yourself or with a team to prepare your heart for God's work in and through you on your trip.

Dearborn, Tim. *Short-Term Missions Workbook: From Mission Tourists to Global Citizens*. Downers Grove, IL: InterVarsity, 2003.

Judge, Cindy. *Before You Pack Your Bag, Prepare Your Heart: 12 Bible Studies for Short-Term Mission Preparation.* Wheaton: Campfire Resources, 2000.

Cross-Cultural Training Tools

These resources provide a way into enhancing your CQ—especially knowledge CQ (understanding cross-cultural differences) and behavioral CQ (acting appropriately cross-culturally).

Elmer, Duane. *Cross-Cultural Connections.* Downers Grove, IL: InterVarsity, 2002.

Kohls, L. Robert, and John Knight. *Developing Intercultural Awareness: A Cross-Cultural Training Handbook.* Yarmouth, ME: Intercultural, 1994.

Lingenfelter, Sherwood. *Agents of Transformation.* Grand Rapids: Baker, 1996.

Morrison, Terri, Wayne Conaway, and George Borden. *Kiss, Bow, or Shake Hands: How to Do Business in Sixty Countries.* Holbrook, MA: Bob Adams, 1994.

Nussbaum, Stan. *The ABC's of American Culture: Understanding the American People through Their Common Sayings.* Colorado Springs: Global Mapping International, 1998.

Storti, Craig. *Cross-Cultural Dialogues: 74 Brief Encounters with Cultural Difference.* Yarmouth, ME: Intercultural, 1994.

———. *The Art of Crossing Cultures.* Yarmouth, ME: Intercultural, 1990.

Follow-Up Tools

As a way to make short-term missions part of our lifelong journey rather than isolated two-week experiences, consider these resources. (Dearborn's tool listed in the "Devotional" tools also includes some follow-up resources.)

Chinn, Lisa Espineli. *Reentry Guide for Short-Term Mission Leaders.* Orlando: Deeper Roots, 1998.

Dearborn. *Short-Term Missions Workbook.*

Delta Ministries. *The Next Mile Project.* Waynesboro, GA: Authentic Media, 2005.

Global Awareness

Here are a few of the many tools available to help you widen your perspective to the issues of our twenty-first-century world. Check out these books and resources.

Ash, Timothy Garton. *Free World: America, Europe, and the Surprising Future of the West.* New York: Random House, 2002.

BBC News. http://news.bbc.co.uk/.

Global Learning Center. Grand Rapids Theological Seminary. http://grts.cornerstone.edu/resources/glc/.

Mission Network News. Cornerstone University. http://www.mnnonline.org/.

Singer, Peter. *One World: The Ethics of Globalization.* New Haven, CT: Yale University Press, 2002.

Cultural Intelligence

Serving with Eyes Wide Open is the first book to apply the relatively new field of CQ to missions. Some of the original resources are listed below. Early, Ang, & Tan's 2006 book includes a self-assessment for CQ in the appendix.

Center for Cultural Intelligence. Nanyang Technological University, Singapore. http://www.cci.ntu.edu.sg/.

Earley, P. Christopher, Ang Soon, and Tan Joo-Seng. *CQ: Cultural Intelligence at Work.* Stanford, CA: Stanford University Press, 2006.

Earley, P. Christopher, and Ang Soon. *Cultural Intelligence: Individual Interactions across Cultures.* Stanford, CA: Stanford University Press, 2003.

Thomas, David, and Kerr Inkson. *Cultural Intelligence: People Skills for Global Business*. San Francisco: Berrett-Koehler, 2004.

Biblical Theology of Missions

The final chapter of *Serving with Eyes Wide Open* begins to present a biblical theology of missions that connects our short-term mission work with the full narrative of Scripture. Some resources to think further about the implications of rooting mission in creation and making the Shema central include:

Intersect. Grand Rapids. http://www.intersectcommunity.com/.

McKnight, Scot. *The Jesus Creed: Loving God, Loving Others*. Brewster, MA: Paraclete, 2004.

Newbigin, Leslie. *The Open Secret: An Introduction to the Theology of Mission*. Grand Rapids: Eerdmans, 1995.

Webber, Robert. *Ancient-Future Evangelism: Making Your Church a Faith-Forming Community*. Grand Rapids: Baker, 2003.

Wittmer, Michael. *Heaven Is a Place on Earth: Why Everything You Do Matters to God*. Grand Rapids: Zondervan, 2004.

Wright, N. T. *The New Testament and the People of God*. Minneapolis: Fortress, 1992.

Notes

Introduction

1. With apologies to my fellow "Americans" who share the American continents with me from Chile to Canada, I've chosen to use the term *American* as it's often used throughout the world—to describe people who are from the United States of America. I've done so for ease in writing and reading. However, I am sympathetic to the idea that the United States is but one country within the Americas!

2. Roger Peterson, Gordon Aeschliman, and R. Wayne Sneed, *Maximum Impact, Short-Term Mission: The God-Commanded Repetitive Deployment of Swift, Temporary Nonprofessional Missionaries* (Minneapolis: STEM, 2003).

3. *Colonialism* refers to a nation exerting its power over places outside its own boundaries. For example, nearly every country in places such as Africa and Southeast Asia was colonized throughout the eighteenth and nineteenth centuries (or before). Colonialism lost most of its ground in the late twentieth century. However, neocolonialism continues—the indirect ways nations or other groups try to dominate other peoples.

4. Historically the Western world was the Hellenistic division of Greeks versus the barbarians in the East, and the Latin-speaking Roman world versus the rest. *West* has long been used to refer to those nations and peoples living in a more so-called developed or civilized way. During the Cold War, the term *West* shifted to refer to NATO nations versus those in the Eastern Bloc, but even that category no longer exists. More recently the term *West* has been used to describe developed nations, in the Eastern Hemisphere (Japan, Singapore, and Australia) as well as in the Western Hemisphere. Increasingly *West* is used today to describe free nations as compared to those still under totalitarian rule.

5. P. Christopher Earley of London Business School and Ang Soon of Nanyang Technical University in Singapore have led the charge on constructing the theory and related research regarding CQ. I'm indebted to Soon in particular, a fellow follower of Christ, who has encouraged me and helped me to adapt this work to missions (see P. Christopher Earley and Ang Soon, *Cultural Intelligence:*

Individual Interactions across Cultures [Stanford, CA: Stanford University Press, 2003], 239).

Chapter 1 One World: Snapshots of the Globe

1. U.S. Census Bureau, "World POPClock Projection," June 17, 2005, http://www.census.gov/ipc/www/popclockworld.html.

2. Anthony Marsella, "Conflict, Negotiation, and Mediation across Cultures" (lecture, Fourth Biennial Conference on Intercultural Research, Kent, OH, May 5, 2005).

3. Timothy Garton Ash, *Free World: America, Europe, and the Surprising Future of the West* (New York: Random House, 2002), 149.

4. Tim Dearborn, "A Global Future for Local Churches," in *The Local Church in a Global Era: Reflections for a New Century*, ed. M. L. Stackhouse, T. Dearborn, and S. Paeth (Grand Rapids: Eerdmans), 212.

5. Richard Dooling, *White Man's Grave* (New York: Picador, 1994), 168.

6. Many of the statistics in this section come from Bryant L. Myers, *Exploring World Mission: Context and Challenges* (Federal Way, WA: World Vision International, 2003).

7. Bruce Huseby, "AIDS/Razor Blades," email message to author, June 18, 2005.

8. United Nations AIDS Report, "Report on the Global AIDS Epidemic" (New York: United Nations, 2004).

9. United States Committee for Refugees, "World Refugee Survey: Refugee and IDP Statistics" (Washington, DC: USCRI, 2004).

10. Bryant L. Myers, "Compassion with an Attitude: A Humanitarian's View of Human Suffering," *Brandywine Review of Faith and International Affairs* 2, no. 3 (Winter 2004–2005): 51–55.

11. Don Golden, "Sierra Leone Refugee," email message to author, March 20, 2002.

12. Ted Fishman, *China Inc.: How the Rise of the Next Superpower Challenges America and the World* (New York: Scribner, 2005), 343.

13. Shawn Tully, "Teens: The Most Global Market of All," *Fortune*, May 16, 1994, 90.

14. Benjamin Barber, *Jihad vs. McWorld: How Globalism and Tribalism Are Reshaping the World* (New York: Ballantine Books, 1996), 9.

15. Lamin Sanneh and Joel Carpenter, eds., *The Changing Face of Christianity: Africa, the West, and the World* (New York: Oxford University Press, 2005), 222.

Chapter 2 One Church: The Changing Face of Christianity

1. Philip Jenkins, *The Next Christendom: The Coming of Global Christianity* (New York: Oxford University Press, 2002), 2.

2. Ibid., 37.

3. I'm on a campaign to eliminate "third world" from our vocabulary altogether. I'm well aware that it's still used broadly by the media and by many ministry leaders. While the etymology of "third world" is not originally negative (first world being the Allied nations who opposed communism, second world

being communist nations, and third world being a third alternative to either capitalism or communism), many people outside the "first" world find the term offensive. "Developed" and "developing" world is better but still connotes that one is ahead of the other. Majority world, a descriptive term of where most of the world lives, is the preferred term by nationals in these regions, or West and non-West as defined elsewhere.

4. Sanneh and Carpenter, *Changing Face of Christianity*, 3.

5. David Barrett and Todd Johnson, eds., *World Christian Trends: AD 30–AD 2200* (Pasadena, CA: William Carey Library, 2001) 3–9.

6. Ibid., 4.

7. Sanneh and Carpenter, *Changing Face of Christianity*, 5.

8. Nina Shea, *In the Lion's Den: A Shocking Account of Persecution and Matrydom of Christians Today and How We Should Respond* (Nashville: Broadman & Holman, 1997), ix.

9. Jenkins, *Next Christendom*, 76.

10. R. Pierce Beaver, "The History of Mission Strategy," in *Perspectives on the World Christian Movement: A Reader*, ed. R. Winter and S. Hawthorne (Pasadena, CA: William Carey Library, 1999), 74.

11. Isaac M. T. Mwase, "Shall They Till with Their Own Hoes? Baptists in Zimbabwe and New Patterns of Interdependence, 1950–2000," in *The Changing Face of Christianity: Africa, the West, and the World*, ed. Lamin Sanneh and Joel Carpenter (New York: Oxford University Press, 2005), 74.

12. Sanneh and Carpenter, *Changing Face of Christianity*, 7.

13. Clinton Arnold, *Powers of Darkness: Principalities and Powers in Paul's Letters* (Downers Grove, IL: InterVarsity), 210.

14. Jenkins, *Next Christendom*, 125.

15. Brother Yun and Paul Hattaway, *The Heavenly Man: The Remarkable Story of Chinese Christian Brother Yun* (Grand Rapids: Monarch, 2003), 65.

16. Paul Hattaway, *Back to Jerusalem: Three Chinese House Church Leaders Share Their Vision to Complete the Great Commission* (Waynesboro, GA: Authentic Media, 2003).

17. Sam George, "The Nation with the Most Missionaries Is India," *Friday Fax*, November 5, 2004.

18. World Evangelical Alliance, "Report on Global Consultation on Evangelical Missiology" (lecture, Global Consultation on Evangelical Missiology, Iguacu, Parana, Brazil, October 1999).

19. Hattaway, *Back to Jerusalem*, xi.

Part 2 Conflicting Images: Americans' vs. Nationals' Perspectives on Short-Term Missions

1. Christian Smith, *Soul Searching: The Religious and Spiritual Lives of American Teenagers* (New York: Oxford University Press, 2005), 69.

2. Organizations use different distinctions to define short-term versus long-term missions. For the most part, long-term missions refers to someone who is going for two years or more to live in another culture and do missions. While short-term missions often includes anything less than two years, this book focuses primarily on short-term mission efforts that last ten days to two weeks.

3. The findings shared in this book from my own research have come from a qualitative method using a grounded-theory approach. Data was collected and analyzed through pretrip and posttrip interviews and journals of North American participants. In addition, the nationals who received the short-term groups were interviewed and completed surveys. Any quotes by short-term participants or nationals without a footnote are from data I've collected. The complete report on the study examining American pastors' training efforts overseas is reported in David Livermore, "The Emperor's New Clothes: Experiences of Stateside Church Leaders Who Train Cross-Culturally" (PhD diss., Michigan State University, 2001).

Chapter 3 Motivation: "Missions Should Be Fun!"

1. Bulletin announcement, in Glenn Schwartz, "Two Awesome Problems: How Short-Term Missions Can Go Wrong," *International Journal of Frontier Missions* 20, no. 4 (2004): 33.

2. Hattaway, *Back to Jerusalem*, 101.

3. The role of our expectations upon how we experience new situations is referred to as "anticipatory socialization." Robert Merton, who initially articulated this theory, examined how the expectations of U.S. Army recruits influenced their experiences as privates. Merton found that those privates who most accurately anticipated and embraced the U.S. Army culture and its values were the privates most likely to experience promotions within the army's hierarchy. I've done some work applying this important theory to examining the role of short-termers' expectations upon their actual engagement in short-term missions (see Robert Merton, *Social Theory and Social Structure* [New York: Free Press, 1968], 319).

4. Peterson, Aeschliman, and Sneed, *Maximum Impact, Short-Term Mission*, 199–210.

5. Byron Shearer, "Mission Trip: A Microcosm of Life," *Vision for Youth Magazine*, Spring 2005, 17, 30.

6. *Group Magazine*, November/December 2004, 39.

7. Schwartz, "Two Awesome Problems," 33.

8. Hattaway, *Back to Jerusalem*, 101.

9. R. Judd, "Do Short-Term Programmes Achieve the Purposes for Which They Were Established?" (PhD diss., London Bible College, 1996), 16, 19; Terence Linhart, "The Curricular Nature of Youth Group Short-Term Cross-Cultural Service Projects" (PhD diss., Purdue University, 2004).

10. Terence Linhart, "They Were So Alive: The Spectacle Self and Youth Group Short-Term Mission Trips" (paper presented at the North Central Evangelical Missiological Society Meeting, Deerfield, IL, April 9, 2005).

11. Christian Smith, *Soul Searching*, 69.

12. Ridge Burns and Noel Bechetti, *The Complete Student Missions Handbook* (Grand Rapids: Zondervan, 1990).

13. Marshall Allen, "International Short-Term Missions: A Divergence from the Great Commission?" *Youthworker Journal* 16 (May/June 2001): 41.

14. Ibid.

15. Linhart, "Curricular Nature"; Kurt VerBeek, "The Impact of Short-Term Missions. A Case Study: House Construction in Honduras after Hurricane Mitch," May 3, 2005, http://www.calvin.edu/academic/sociology/staff/kurt.htm.

16. David Maclure, "Wholly Available? Missionary Motivation where Consumer Choice Reigns," William Carey, 2001, http://www.williamcarey.org.uk/FILES/essay1.htm.

17. Jeff Edmondson, "The End of the Youth Mission Trip as We Know It," *Youthworker Journal* 16 (May/June 2001): 30–34.

18. Reported from a fellow missionary to JoAnn VanEngen, "The Cost of Short-Term Missions," *The Other Side* (January/February 2000), 20.

19. VerBeek, "Impact of Short-Term Missions."

Chapter 4 Urgency: "Just Do It!"

1. Dooling, *White Man's Grave*, 146.

2. Robert Webber, *The Younger Evangelicals: Facing the Challenges of the New World* (Grand Rapids: Baker, 2002), 41.

3. Peterson, Aeschliman, and Sneed, *Maximum Impact, Short-Term Mission*, 29.

4. Rob Bell, "Jesus is Difficult," part 3 (sermon, Mars Hill Bible Church, Grandville, MI, April 17, 2005).

Chapter 5 Common Ground: "They Don't Fly Planes in India When It Rains"

1. Earley and Soon, *Cultural Intelligence*, 239.

2. Paul H. Ray and Sherry Ruth Anderson, *The Cultural Creatives: How Fifty Million People Are Changing the World* (New York: Three Rivers, 2001), 41.

3. Linhart, "They Were So Alive," 7.

4. Ibid.

5. Stuart Hall, *Representation: Cultural Representation and Signifying Practices* (Thousand Oaks, CA: SAGE, 1997).

Chapter 6 The Bible: "Just Stick to the Bible and You Can't Go Wrong!"

1. Jacob Loewen, "The Gospel: Its Content and Communication," in *Down to Earth: Studies in Christianity and Culture*, ed. J. Stott and R. Coote (Grand Rapids: Eerdmans, 1980), 121.

2. Stan Grenz and John Franke, *Beyond Foundationalism: Shaping Theology in a Postmodern Context* (Louisville: Westminster John Knox, 2001), 39.

3. *Bibliolatry* is a term often used to describe the worship of the Bible over and above worship of Jesus himself.

4. I explore this further in my book *Connecting Your Journey with the Story of God: Disciplemaking in Diverse Contexts* (Elburn, IL: Sonlife Ministries, 2001).

5. Brian McLaren, *A New Kind of Christian: A Tale of Two Friends on a Spiritual Journey* (San Francisco: Jossey-Bass, 2001), 52.

6. Michael Horton, ed., *A Confessing Theology for Postmodern Times* (Wheaton: Crossway, 2001), 96.

7. Ibid., 99.

8. N. T. Wright, *The Challenge of Jesus: Rediscovering Who Jesus Was and Is* (Downers Grove, IL: InterVarsity, 1999) 181.

9. I discuss this further in my book *Connecting Your Journey with the Story of God*.

10. Arthur Patzia, *The Emergence of the Church: Context, Growth, Leadership, and Worship* (Downers Grove, IL: InterVarsity, 2001), 13.

11. My GRTS colleague Gary Meadors provides some helpful perspective and tools for applying Scripture to our current contexts in his book *Decision Making God's Way* (Grand Rapids: Baker, 2003) 104–26.

12. Aida Besancon Spencer and William David Spencer, eds., *The Global God: Multicultural Evangelical Views of God* (Grand Rapids: Baker, 1998).

13. Leslie Newbigin, *The Open Secret: An Introduction to the Theology of Mission* (Grand Rapids: Eerdmans. 1995).

14. Mark Noll, back cover of *The Global God: Multicultural Evangelical Views of God*, ed. Aida Besancon Spencer and William David Spencer (Grand Rapids: Baker, 1998), 282.

Chapter 7 Money: "They're So Happy"

1. Brad Pitt, interview by Diane Sawyer, *Primetime Live*, ABC News, June 7, 2005.

2. Ibid.

3. Simon Robinson, "Do They Know It's Simplistic? Band-Aid's Intentions Are Good but Africa Needs More than Just a Christmas Jingle," *Time*, November 28, 2004, http://www.time.com/time/europe/.

4. Schwartz, "Two Awesome Problems," 32.

5. VanEngen, "Cost of Short-Term Missions," 21.

6. Ibid., 22.

7. Schwartz, "Two Awesome Problems," 28.

8. Shane Claiborne, "Downward Mobility in an Upscale World," *The Other Side* (November/December 2000), 11.

9. Dooling, *White Man's Grave*, 157.

10. Max Van Manen, "Moral Language and Pedagogical Experience," *Journal of Curriculum Studies* 32, no. 2 (March/April 2000): 315–27.

11. Linhart, "They Were So Alive," 6.

12. Ibid., 9.

13. VanEngen, "Cost of Short-Term Missions," 22.

Chapter 8 Simplicity: "You're Either for Us or against Us!"

1. President George W. Bush, transcript of address to joint session of congress, CNN, September 20, 2001, http://archives.cnn.com/2001/US/09/20/gen. bush.transcript/.

2. Jefferson Morley, "Michael Moore, Ugly American: Filmmaker Taken to Task for Arrogance, Ignoring Israel," *Washington Post*, July 13, 2004.

3. Linhart, "They Were So Alive," 6.

4. Ibid., 10.

5. R. Slimbach, "First, Do No Harm: Short-Term Missions at the Dawn of a New Millennium," *Evangelical Missions Quarterly* 36, no. 4 (October 2000): 432.

6. Linhart, "Curricular Nature," 190–91.

Part 3 Sharpening Our Focus and Service with Cultural Intelligence (CQ)

1. David Livermore, personal journal, June 25, 2003.

2. P. Christopher Earley of London Business School and Ang Soon of Naynang Business School in Singapore developed CQ as a framework for nurturing effective cross-cultural interactions. The focus of their work has been upon the cross-cultural interactions of those in the business world and the hospitality industry. I've had the privilege of interacting with Ang Soon a number of times and am grateful for her help in encouraging me to adapt CQ for use in the missions arena (see Earley and Soon, *Cultural Intelligence*).

3. The case study of college students traveling to Shanghai is fictitious, though it was developed using my research on short-term experiences.

Chapter 9 Seek to Understand: Knowledge CQ

1. A portion of this material was adapted from Kenneth Cushner and R. W. Brislin, *Intercultural Interactions: A Practical Guide* (Thousand Oaks, CA: SAGE, 1996).

2. Geert Hofstede, *Cultures and Organizations: Software of the Mind* (New York: McGraw-Hill, 1997), 5.

3. Robert Levine, *A Geography of Time: The Temporal Misadventures of a Social Psychologist, or How Every Culture Keeps Time Just a Little Bit Differently* (New York: Basic, 1997).

4. P. Christopher Earley, Ang Soon, and Tan Joo-Seng, *CQ: Cultural Intelligence at Work* (Stanford, CA: Stanford University Press, 2006).

5. Edward Hall and M. R. Hall, *Understanding Cultural Differences: Germans, French, and Americans* (Yarmouth, ME: Intercultural, 1990).

6. Hofstede explored five different dimensions that help expose cultural differences—individualism, power distance, uncertainty avoidance, masculinity, and long-term orientation. The first three are the most useful for developing knowledge CQ (see Geert Hofstede, *Culture's Consequences: International Differences in Work-Related Values* [Newbury Park, CA: SAGE, 1980]).

7. L. Robert Kohls and John Knight, *Developing Intercultural Awareness: A Cross-Cultural Training Handbook* (Yarmouth, ME: Intercultural, 1994), 44.

8. Ibid., 45.

9. Adapted from Hall and Hall, *Understanding Cultural Differences*; Levine, *Geography of Time*; and Hofstede, *Culture's Consequences*.

10. Riki Takeuchi, Paul Tesluk, and Sophia Marinova, "Role of International Experiences in the Development of Cultural Intelligence" (paper presented at the Academy of Management, New Orleans, LA, August 11, 2004).

11. David Thomas and Kerr Inkson, *Cultural Intelligence: People Skills for Global Business* (San Francisco: Berrett-Koehler, 2004), 19.

Chapter 10 On Second Thought: Interpretive CQ

1. Ang Soon, personal communication with the author, April 22, 2005.
2. Thomas and Inkson, *Cultural Intelligence*, 52.
3. Adapted from Keith Ferrazzi's use of the Johari window in his business book on networking (see Keith Ferrazzi, *Never Eat Alone: And Other Secrets to Success, One Relationship at a Time* [New York: Random House, 2005], 154).
4. Takeuchi, Tesluk, and Marinova, "Role of International Experiences."
5. Kenneth Cushner, *Beyond Tourism: A Practical Guide to Meaningful Educational Travel* (Lanham, MD: Scarecrow Educational, 2004), 45.

Chapter 11 Try, Try Again: Perseverance CQ

1. Earley and Soon, *Cultural Intelligence*, 124.
2. Earley, Soon, and Joo-Seng, *CQ: Cultural Intelligence at Work*.
3. When we do this, we engage in what marriage counselors call "idealistic distortion"—the tendency to see something in an overly positive manner and to believe that rose-colored view is reality. Sometimes marriages are eroding, but the husband is in such denial, he sees the marriage as he longs for it to be, even though that isn't close to reality. We often do this with our short-term mission experiences.

Chapter 12 Actions Speak Louder than Words: Behavioral CQ

1. Earley and Soon, *Cultural Intelligence*, 5.

Chapter 13 The Heart of the Matter: Shema

1. N. T. Wright, *Following Jesus: Biblical Reflections on Discipleship* (Grand Rapids: Eerdmans, 1994), 10.
2. David Livermore and Steve Argue, *Explore 1: Shepherd through Following* (Grand Rapids: Intersect, 2005) 6–7.
3. Kenda Creasy Dean, *Practicing Passion: Youth and the Quest for a Passionate Church* (Grand Rapids: Eerdmans, 2004), 192–93.
4. Henry Nouwen, *In the Name of Jesus: Reflections on Christian Leadership* (New York: Crossroad, 1989).
5. Jonathan Edwards, "Thoughts on the Revival of Religion in New England," in *The Works of Jonathan Edwards*, vol. 1 (Carlisle, PA: Banner of Truth Trust, 1834), 380.
6. Chip Huber, "Building a Community Bridge across the World: The God-Engineered Link between Chicago and Zambia," *Youthworker Journal* 20, no. 4 (July/August 2005): 46–49.
7. Newbigin, *Open Secret*, 174.
8. David Stoner, "The Missional Church Is Passionately 'Glocal': A North American Perspective," *Connections*, March 2005.

David A. Livermore (PhD, Michigan State University) is executive director of the Global Learning Center at Grand Rapids Theological Seminary and is cofounder of Intersect, a ministry that provides leadership training and consulting to emerging leaders in ministries around the world.

Also by David Livermore

Cultural Intelligence
IMPROVING YOUR CQ TO ENGAGE OUR MULTICULTURAL WORLD
by Dave Livermore
9780801035890   288 pp.

Twenty-first-century society is diverse, and Christians must be able to understand other cultures and communicate effectively between and among them. This new addition to the Youth, Family, and Culture series explores the much-needed skill of Cultural Intelligence (CQ), the ability to work effectively across national, ethnic, and even organizational cultures.

While rooted in sound, scholarly research, *Cultural Intelligence* is highly practical and accessible to general readers. It will benefit students as well as guide ministry leaders interested in increasing their cultural awareness and sensitivity. Packed with assessment tools, simulations, case studies, and exercises, *Cultural Intelligence* will help transform individuals and organizations into effective intercultural communicators of the gospel.

Baker Academic
a division of Baker Publishing Group
www.BakerAcademic.com